INTRODUCTION TO EDUCATION
Series editor: Jonathan Solity

THE CHALLENGE FOR TEACHERS

THE CHALLENGE FOR TEACHERS

John Eggleston

CASSELL

Cassell
Villiers House   387 Park Avenue South
41/47 Strand   New York, NY 10016-8810
London WC2N 5JE   USA

British Library Cataloguing-in-Publication Data
A catalogue record for this book is available from the
British Library.

ISBN 0-304-32368-3 (hardback)
      0-304-32369-1 (paperback)

Library of Congress Cataloging-in-Publication Data
Eggleston, John, 1926–
    The challenge for teachers / John Eggleston.
      p. cm. – (Introduction to education)
    Includes bibliographical references and index.
    ISBN 0-304-32368-3 – ISBN 0-304-32369-1
(pbk.)
      1. Teachers–Great Britain. I. Title. II. Series:
Introduction to education (New York, N.Y.)
LB1775.4.G7E44 1992
371.1'00941–dc20   91-23925
                                             CIP

Typeset by Colset Private Limited, Singapore
Printed and bound in Great Britain by
Biddles Ltd, Guildford and King's Lynn

CONTENTS

To Gillian

FOREWORD

The 1980s and 1990s have witnessed unprecedented changes to the education system. These have had a dramatic impact, particularly in relation to:

- schools' relationships with parents and the community;
- the funding and management of schools;
- the curriculum;
- the assessment of children's learning.

It can be an extremely daunting task for student teachers to unravel the details and implications of these initiatives. This Introduction to Education series therefore offers a comprehensive analysis and evaluation of educational theory and practice in the light of recent developments.

The series examines topics and issues of concern to those entering the teaching profession. Major themes representing a spectrum of educational opinion are presented in a clear, balanced and analytic manner.

The authors in the series are authorities in their field. They emphasize the need to have a well-informed and critical teaching profession and present a positive and optimistic view of the teacher's role. They endorse the view that teachers have a significant influence over the extent to which any legislation or ideology is translated into effective classroom practice.

Each author addresses similar issues, which can be summarized as:

- presenting and debating theoretical perspectives within appropriate social, political, and educational contexts
- identifying key arguments
- identifying individuals who have made significant contributions to the field under review
- discussing and evaluating key legislation
- critically evaluating research and highlighting implications for classroom practice
- providing an overview of the current state of debate within each field
- describing the features of good practice

The books are written primarily for student teachers. However, they will be of interest and value to all those involved in education.

Jonathan Solity
Series Editor

PREFACE

In this book I have tried to relate the momentous events in education in recent years to the fundamental issues that underlie them. The challenge of doing this in a way that will be accessible and immediately helpful is welcome – you, the reader, will judge how successful I have been. I am grateful to the publishers and the series editor, Jonathan Solity, for the stimulus to undertake this task. They have been helpful throughout, as have my other colleagues at the University of Warwick. Margaret Handy has kindly prepared the manuscript through several drafts. I am grateful to them all – but I accept total responsibility for all the faults of the final product. Naomi Roth and Fiona McKenzie at Cassell have been outstandingly helpful: I owe them a considerable debt!

John Eggleston

CHAPTER 1

Being a teacher

OVERVIEW

This chapter considers what it is to be a teacher in modern society and reviews the professionalism and status of teachers.

Key teacher tasks
- Earning and keeping professional status.
- Learning the context in which one works and being sensitive to it.
- Achieving 'inner directedness' rather than 'other-directedness'.
- Becoming not only a competent teacher but also a curriculum expert, manager, assessor and guardian of opportunity.

To be a teacher is like living a life dedicated to mission impossible. To begin to satisfy the complex demands loaded on to teachers by governments, parents, employers, children and society at large is unthinkable. Even if the demands were compatible and feasible it would take several lifetimes of schooling to achieve them – and social change would make some aspects of the task obsolete even before they were attempted. Yet despite this, the satisfactions of teaching can be immense: no other profession can experience the immediate joy of children's new learning, understanding and fulfilment or see the long-term results of the commitments, enthusiasm and careers that are formed in the school.

PROFESSIONALISM

Even in the first paragraph teaching has been labelled a profession. It has most of the necessary characteristics, such as a high level of responsibility for the lives of others, duties governed by agreed rules of conduct, restriction of entry to those who are recognized as trained, qualified and experienced and a social status that is determined by the nature of the employment rather than by the individual as a person. Yet there are problems with the professional status of teachers that are not experienced by most other professional groups. Teachers lack the social distance enjoyed by doctors and lawyers. Every citizen has spent at least ten years in close encounters with teachers. Doctors and lawyers can use knowledge inaccessible to the public and work on a specialized 'stage set' such as the surgery, the court room or the consulting room to command instant respect and status. In schools teachers have to – and wish to – establish close relationships with their pupils; they share their expertise with them and work in an environment that very soon becomes wholly familiar and unawesome.

There are other differences too. Teachers are by far the most numerous profession; most communities have teachers in residence. Unlike any other professionals, teachers are always outnumbered by their clients, usually by thirty or more to one. The task of maintaining the authority necessary to control the behaviour of pupils in order to achieve conditions for effective learning makes the work of a teacher immensely more difficult than that of any other professional person. Yet a further difficulty is that teachers do not have the set of rewards and penalties with which other professions can influence their relationships with clients. Teachers cannot offer their pupils the prospect of life instead of death, freedom instead of imprisonment, welfare instead of destitution. Teachers' 'clients' do not always feel that they are benefiting by their treatment – often quite the reverse!

THE STATUS OF TEACHERS

In modern society, teachers have a problem of status. Because everybody has at one time been at school, most people believe that they themselves have at least some or even most of a teacher's expertise and capability: 'anybody could teach those children'. Because they are so familiar, teachers lack the mystique that normally enhances professional status and power, and are subject to public attempts to control and constrain them: by legislation, public opinion and even, occasionally, by media ridicule and prejudice.

An immediate consequence of all this is to be seen in the pay of teachers. Because of the public evaluation of their work, teachers in most Western countries cannot achieve the generally high salaries of other professionals. And because teachers are so numerous and so familiar, the organizations representing them on both sides of the Atlantic are increasingly driven to techniques used by organized labour unions, such as mass or selective strike action. Not only does this entail hardship for their clients (the very antithesis of professional conduct) but it also links teachers to the image of workers' unions. This contrasts with the situation of medical and legal professionals, whose associations win public support through manipulative public relations campaigns reinforcing the notion that the public need their specialist expertise. In contrast, teachers' pay negotiations have often diminished their status relative to the other professions. Recent attempts to 'privatize' teaching by separating education into school units rather than local authority or school board groupings may have important consequences upon pay bargaining and may reverse the trend to teacher unionization. Some politicians envisage giving all schools the right to negotiate the salaries of all their teachers, as most 'public' and private schools do already.

The consequences of teachers' marginal professional status are familiar. Politicians, journalists and letter writers unhesitatingly attribute many of the problems of society to the work of teachers. Public debates on, say, abortion law commonly have approximately equal members of both sides complaining of too much sex education in the schools, or too little. Major employers, often in a single speech, complain of too little attention to the basic skills – and also of teachers' failure to make children aware of electronic calculators and word processors. A correspondent in a British national newspaper in 1990 held teachers responsible for an alleged increase in 'motiveless murders'. He commented, 'schools have long failed to teach the values of restraint and concern for others'. The list is endless; teachers can be blamed for vandalism, industrial strikes, impoliteness, litter on the streets and almost any other social behaviour that can be objected to.

THE CONTEXT OF TEACHING

How can any teacher, faced with such a barrage of advice, exhortation and criticism, continue with 'mission impossible' and reach the real achievements and results of teaching? This book attempts to show the way. It will look at the social context of teaching and show how the teacher can understand the social forces that surround the classroom and seek to use them rather than to be used, or even abused, by them. It will look at the role of the teacher and contrast the conventional model of the 'good' teacher and the 'good' pupil with the reality of what is possible and worthwhile. It will look at the ways in which the expectations and requirements of employers, government and communities are formed and imposed and how teachers may seek to interpret or even exploit these requirements to enhance rather than hinder their work.

It will look at the social backgrounds of pupils and discuss how

3

their class, gender and racial background may already have brought about differences in their achievements, aspirations and 'self images'. Teachers have the opportunity to build on children's pre-school and home background experience in different ways. They may do so negatively, and so reinforce divisions and disadvantages that come about through thoughtlessness or prejudice, or do so positively by maximizing children's capabilities and achieving fuller equality of opportunity in schooling.

The book will also look at what is taught in the classroom, what determines the formal curriculum and to whom it is made available, and how it is used to determine the life chances of the children who receive it. The introduction of national curricula in England and Wales and elsewhere will be viewed in this context. The operation of the 'hidden curriculum' (the understandings that underlie classroom life and perhaps offer the most permanent learning of all) will also be considered.

ASSESSING THE WORK OF CHILDREN

The book also considers assessment and suggests some ways of improving matters in this connection. Parents and employers have a right to know what children are achieving and how they are being taught. Teachers can also benefit by keeping parents and others beyond the school better informed, if only to refute the unsubstantiated assumptions that have already been mentioned. Sadly teachers have often been unsuccessful in this respect. The writer, a parent of four children in the state system, has frequently attended parents' evenings. Often, after a long wait to see the relevant teacher, he has been shown his child's mark record and told that the child was 'doing well, average marks seven out of ten'. But this is meaningless information unless it is accompanied by information about the task: its nature and level, the teacher's marking standards, the norm for the class, and much else.

In Britain and most other Western countries new legislation now imposes complex assessment procedures upon schools and teachers; such procedures are essential if national curricula are to be imposed effectively by national governments. This book considers how teachers may turn these complex, time-consuming requirements into activities that may enhance their work and their recognition. But above all, the discussion on assessment, in Chapter 8 and elsewhere, will consider how teachers can achieve self-assessment, because only in this way can they break out from 'other-directedness' and achieve 'inner-directedness' that allows them to achieve true professionalism and to claim the status and power they need to tackle the work expected of them.

The book will also look at the ways in which teachers, right from the earliest years of schooling, prepare young people for work and adult life, helping them to turn their accrued learning and understanding into adult roles and status in ways that are fulfilling, realistic and satisfying. Even the most effective schooling is of little value if it cannot be converted into a successful, worthwhile adult lifestyle.

A final chapter will explore the teacher's role as a manager – a member of the school management team and largely in control of classroom management: curriculum, teaching style, resources and the creation of an optimal learning environment for all the children.

In these considerations of the nature of teaching, of the teacher's multiple role as curriculum expert, classroom manager, guardian of opportunity and assessor, the book forms an accompaniment to the other volumes in the series, which each deal in detail with specific activities or responsibilities of teachers. Not only will it examine modern teachers' roles and the social stage on which they are played but it will also analyse how they may be played in a way that is effective and satisfying for teachers and learners. Attention will also be given to the negative analyses of teaching (some of them springing from teachers themselves) that have done much to inhibit recruitment and retention of teachers. In short, the book will offer a realistic appraisal of the oldest profession, which, despite popular mythology, is not prostitution but teaching.

RECOMMENDED READING

The New Teacher in School (HMI, 1988), though an official report and as such somewhat austere and official, contains a good deal of useful information.

Martin Powell and Jonathan Solity, *Teachers in Control* (London: Routledge, 1990) goes into useful detail about the pressures under which teachers operate and suggests ways in which they can 'recover the freedom to make their own decisions'.

Les Bell, *Appraising Teachers in Schools* (London: Routledge, 1988) has some very good sections on self-appraisal and team appraisal and also alerts teachers to what others expect of them. Parts make formidable reading – but don't be put off!

Robin Richardson, *Daring to Be a Teacher* (Stoke-on-Trent: Trentham Books, 1990) is an inspiring, sensitive book on being a teacher. It contains many 'parables' – including Richardson's well-known 'elephant' story.

CHAPTER 2

Issues of social class, gender and race

OVERVIEW

This chapter reviews the ways in which differences in social class, gender and race can influence children's achievement. It reviews key concepts of socialization, inner- and other-directedness, restricted and elaborated language codes and social and cultural reproduction. In particular it outlines how positive rather than passive teacher roles may be achieved.

Key teacher tasks

- Trying to ensure that one discovers the capabilities of all children.
- Taking care that one's judgements are not influenced by negative expectations about social class, gender or race.
- Building upon what capabilities the children already have, never suggesting that what they bring (especially in the way of language) is valueless.
- Remembering that differences established or reinforced in school may determine almost all aspects of a child's future and, collectively, play a large part in determining future social structure.

Children come to school with different physical, mental and emotional capabilities. They also come with a bewildering variety of expectations and attitudes that may enhance or diminish the full realization of their capability. These expectations and attitudes are largely a product of their social background and spring from the value systems of their parents, their extended families and the adults and other children in their communities. They are important not only because they have a formative effect on the children but also because they interact with the expectations and attitudes of teachers. Often teachers, despite much effort to the contrary, end up by reinforcing the differentiating consequences of these underlying values, not infrequently to the disadvantage of children.

There are three main categories into which these underlying value systems, with their representative attitudes and expectations, may be placed: social class, gender, and race. Each of these areas is considered in detail in other volumes in this series. Here their effect on work in the classroom and hence their crucial importance in the work of the teacher is examined.

SOCIAL CLASS

A clear example is provided at the outset of schooling. Let us imagine two children entering school from different ends of the social class structure. They are coming into the reception class of a first school serving a catchment area that spans the social spectrum.

On the first morning Kate, from an affluent suburban home, arrives with Kylie, from a much less affluent inner-city family. They enter a well-equipped modern classroom supervised by a teacher who is enthusiastic to help all the children in her class to maximize their capability. Yet Kate will start with many advantages. She will be familiar with the equipment, having almost certainly met it in her home and pre-school playgroup. She will be relaxed with teachers, as she and her parents are likely to know teachers socially and to 'speak the same language'. So she is likely to use her new environment effectively and immediately and to be posting the bricks in the correct slots in the postbox without waiting to be asked. Meanwhile, Kylie has probably been sent to school with the injunction 'Make sure you do what the teacher tells you', and is waiting patiently for the teacher to tell her when to use the unfamiliar equipment for the first time. It is very difficult for the teacher, armed with her developmental checklist, to resist evaluating Kate as 'bright and quick' and Kylie as 'dull and slow' in the first few hours, when the crucial early (and often persistent) diagnoses are made. The diagnosis is very likely to be reinforced by Kate's greater familiarity with books in the home and the strong probability that her parents have already taught her to read.

GENDER

Similar pre-judgements are all too easy to make on gender issues. Boys, encouraged in home and community to be more dominant, assertive and adventurous and to enjoy approval for such behaviour, will behave differently in the classroom from girls, who have often received a very different early encouragement. In particular, as most teachers acknowledge, boys tend to be much more effective in claiming teachers' attention, with predictable consequences for teachers' evaluation.

RACE

Much the same can happen when children from different ethnic backgrounds enter the classroom: their different languages and cultural backgrounds may make it less easy for them to relate to the 'mainstream' knowledge and understanding they are offered. In consequence their achievement may be seen to be lower and their capabilities in their own home language and culture may go unrecognized. The point is well made by Francis O'Reilly, writing in *The Independent* on 13 September 1990:

> The Maths teacher introduces the student teacher to the class and briefs her. Before leaving, she points out a girl sitting on the back row and says, 'Oh, by the way, Jhamari won't understand anything. Give her some additions to do.'
> In French, where they have to label parts of the body, Jhamari steals a glance at her neighbour's book and earns the snarling response, 'Buzz off, stop copying!' In Humanities they are discussing the Reformation and Jhamari is asked to draw a picture of Henry VIII. In science 'sir' need not keep a wary eye on her as she sits, mute, devoid of mischief and curiosity. She goes from class to class in a dream – eyes not fearful or expectant, but dead.
> Jhamari is not handicapped or mentally disturbed. She is simply Bengali. She and many like her go through the school day and the school year as through a great sterile desert, uncomprehending, shut off, neither gaining nor giving. What potential they have is never realized, because it goes unrecognized . . .
> The presence of silent passengers in the classroom means a failure of education, wasted childhoods and demoralized or desensitized teachers. It should at very least become an immediate focus of research, debate and policy.

The crucial point in these three simplified examples of class, gender and race is that whilst the capability and potential of the children may be similar, the teacher's evaluation is likely to be different and to have crucial consequences in subsequent actual achievement. This is because of the formative nature both of children's self-image and of teachers' expectations. In addition, other children in the classroom are quick to reinforce the teacher's expectations. These self-fulfilling prophecies form a central theme of subsequent chapters.

We must emphasize very strongly, however, that this is not an argument for 'putting down' middle-class children, boys or white pupils. There is no place in the classroom for negative experiences. Advantaged children must build on their advantage; the disadvantaged must be given full opportunity to match them by whatever means the teachers can make available.

SOCIALIZATION

An underlying reason for the differences between children before and during schooling is the process of socialization that occurs in family, community and school (and continues through adult life), in which new members of society learn the culture – the values, attitudes, language and general life skills – that enables them to survive. It is an essential process of growth, but unlike physical growth social growth does not occur 'automatically'; it has to be learned from other human beings. And whilst there are aspects of common culture that virtually all members of society know and share, such as language, diet, religion and law, very many aspects are specific to groups within it. These sub-cultures, with recurring variations from the mainstream culture, can lead to widely varying life chances and prospects. And of course the main sub-cultures in virtually all societies are those of social class, gender and race.

There are certainly many others, usually less permanent, such as the sub-cultures of a workplace, a club, a school, or even a school class. Human beings commonly put a great deal of effort into learning the appropriate culture patterns of social groups in which they find themselves or which they aspire to join. Unless they succeed they will never have the recognition of full membership and as a result will be confined to low, marginal roles and status or will even be 'outsiders'. All teachers know children who never quite 'make it' in classroom acceptability and have seen the distress and anxiety such children experience.

The process of learning the culture or sub-culture is known as socialization, and it is a process which can bring individuals together in behaviour and opportunity – or differentiate them.

For many years teachers have reinforced not only the learning of common culture but also the process of differential socialization, helping middle-class children to become middle-class adults, boys to be men and girls to be women and, often, ethnic minority community children to occupy marginal adult roles. More recently, however, teachers have come to see more clearly that this process can lead not only to a kind of social stability but also to great injustice. It can lead to some children receiving status and power beyond their capabilities and others being denied the opportunity to use their capabilities fully. It is a fundamental assumption of this book that teachers wish to maximize the full capability of all their pupils. There are many reasons but three will suffice:

- justice to young people;
- the needs of all modern societies for developed human capability;
- the professional satisfaction of the teachers themselves.

LANGUAGE

Let us now look at some aspects of socialization particularly relevant to the teacher. One is language. We are in debt to Basil Bernstein for reminding us that there are two strikingly different kinds of language usage. His famous story (1961) of the two children on the bus is well known. There are many versions, but all involve two mothers and their equal concern for the safety of their respective children when the bus moves off. Mother A says, 'Sit down now, darling'. Her child says, 'Why?' and mother explains the risk of falling over in careful, detailed ways. After several more 'whys' mother is close to discussing centrifugal force. But when the bus actually moves she has to turn her request into a command. Mother B also asks her child to sit down, faced with 'Why?' she responds with 'I told you to sit down' and soon reaches 'If you don't sit down I'll knock your head off'.

In Bernstein's terminology, child A is being helped to acquire an elaborated code, with complex syntax and extended vocabulary so that eventually every subtlety of meaning can be expressed by words alone. It is a language that middle-class parents use in work and leisure, but also, more crucially, it is the language of the classroom, the textbook and the examination room. Without it success in mainstream education is difficult, even impossible. Child B is experiencing a restricted code of language, one with simple syntax and limited vocabulary. Full meaning requires the words to be augmented by gesture, expression or context. A good example is the building site, where workers may often employ the 'f' word for almost every adjectival or adverbial use, and yet achieve full communication. There are countless restricted codes; almost every permanent social group has its own. Most families have their own version and their use plays an important role in family bonding.

Yet teachers' preferences for elaborated codes, though understandable and largely necessary, should not lead them into the easy belief that these are always superior to restricted codes. Many films and novels have shown that restricted codes can convey, with non-verbal augmentation, a full range of subtle meanings.

Labov made the point clearly in his study (1969) of New York children. He showed that many had been identified by their teachers as being virtually without language capability and that test results confirmed this view. Such children were seen by teachers as virtually ineducable and their schooling had little prospect. The children responded with low motivation, low attendance and low co-operation with their teachers. Yet when Labov mixed with the children out of school he found that in their language they were able to conduct extended discussions and arguments involving complex issues of sport, popular music, commuity relationships, often much more demanding than the verbal reasoning required of them in the class-room. Yet sadly this capability remained unrecognized in their school-ing and its assessment. It does not take many comments such as 'You cannot use that language in the classroom' to turn children into non-verbal members of the class. This point was recognized in the recommendations for the National Curriculum made by the Working Group on English, which urged teachers not to be over-insistent on the use of standard English at all times. Not surprisingly, the recommen-dation led to wide controversy.

SOCIAL CONTROL

But the work of Bernstein and Labov alerts us not only to how language is used but to the significant consequences of its different uses. This is an issue of control. Child A on the bus was not only learning how to use elaborated language but also learning that by understanding and reason it is possible to control one's relationship with the environment and to use it to personal advantage. Child B was learning that personal behaviour is controlled by others; personal understanding is unneces-sary, even irrelevant. The experiences point to different future life-styles, lifestyles probably very similar to those of the children's parents: one based on ability to control situations and having power over others, the other based on being controlled by others. To use con-ceptual terms, the difference is between learning inner-directedness and other-directedness. Using our concept of socialization, it could also be seen as the difference between two distinct patterns of anticipatory socialization.

Most teachers recognize the importance of inner-directedness. It is after all, as we have seen, a crucial element of the teacher's own role. Similarly, all children need to feel they can control some parts of their own lives and enjoy their own 'space'. If children are precluded from, or feel unable to respond to, the opportunities the teacher is offering them for personal space and control, then they are likely to set up alternative sub-cultures in which they can achieve it, as Labov's work clearly shows. For this reason teachers are often faced with the 'anti-group' in schools who find ways of 'counting for something' by adopting deviant, teacher-provoking ways of dress, hairstyle, language or behaviour which may be matched by delinquent and deviant behaviour out of school (e.g. Patrick, 1973).

11

REINFORCING EXPECTATIONS

This discussion of language has focused on social class differences, though in the case of Labov's study the ethnic factor is also relevant since many of the children were black. Brandis and Henderson's study of primary schools (1974) found that, contrary to widespread expectations, parents from all social backgrounds were actively interested in teachers' views of their children and paid keen attention to them. However, there was a marked difference in the response of parents from different social groups. Middle-class parents faced with a less than enthusiastic commentary on their children sought to change the appraisal by giving extra assistance and support to the children and seeking to encourage the teachers to change their views. Working-class parents were equally concerned but tended to defer to the view of the teacher as the expert and to accept the situation. The inevitable consequence was a widening class gap as the differentiation was reaffirmed and built upon. Following the 1988 Education Reform Act and the 1992 Citizen's Charter, all parents in England and Wales will now receive regular information on their children's achievements in National Curriculum subjects. It will be vital for teachers to ensure that all parents are helped to respond effectively to the information they receive.

Many other writers have reaffirmed the class, gender and racial differentiation that is arbitrarily built up and that rapidly assumes permanent dimensions. Douglas (1964) documented how teachers' class-linked perceptions of children of similar ability led to wide variations in actual achievement through the period of primary education. Jackson and Marsden (1960) noted how schools handicapped parents who had little knowledge of the school curriculum and examinations by failing to recognize and remedy their need for better information, thereby diminishing their capability to support and guide their children's education or even to ask appropriate questions.

Delamont (1986), like many other writers, has shown how the expectations teachers hold about the education of girls are different from those they hold about boys and lead to familiar differences in subject choice. In every university the results are clearly to be seen on degree day: very few women receive degrees in engineering and technology, and not infrequently the lone woman engineering graduate receives a special round of applause, much as would be received by a severely handicapped student! Sex stereotypes abound throughout education: 'Boys don't cry', 'Girls don't get dirty'. All readers will know these and many similar exhortations; they are indeed part of the culture of our society and as such are highly formative. We shall return to this theme in our chapter on the roles of children at school.

Eggleston *et al.* (1986) in a study of black young people and their parents showed how teachers underestimated and undervalued the capability and motivation of black children, even though in many cases the schools themselves had reliable evidence of it. In several of the schools the researchers investigated, able black children were assigned to lower-achieving groups; when challenged, teachers argued that this was done 'for social reasons'. At the heart of the 'reasons' were expectations that black children lacked the persistence, ambition and endurance to 'make it' academically, assumptions that the research team demonstrated to be unfounded.

Eggleston and Sadler (1988) in a study of technical and vocational education found that schools were disappointed that black children and their parents were not more enthusiastic about the new opportunities on offer. But the research found that relatively little information was effectively reaching the parents: letters sent home with pupils were often not reaching the home, and even when they did, the letters' standard, formal English was often interpreted inaccurately or incompletely to the parents by the pupils. Conversely, the schools were receiving little or no information about the aspirations of parents and their support for education through such means as supplementary schooling or books and computers in the home. Thus erroneous assumptions about the lack of black parents' enthusiasm and support went unchallenged and once again formed the basis for decisions on examination entry, school reports and, thereby, life prospects. Smith and Tomlinson (1989) present clear evidence that, when schools break through these assumptions, the achievement of *all* pupils, white and black, can be enhanced and that the key variable is good teaching, not race. Much the same conclusion about social class is recorded by Mortimore *et al.* (1987):

> Those schools which were effective for one group tended to be effective for the other. Conversely, those which were ineffective for one group were also usually ineffective for the other. Our results show, therefore, that effective schools tend to 'jack up' the progress of all pupils, irrespective of their social class background, while ineffective schools will usually depress the progress of all pupils.

One of the main reasons for the perpetuation of the negative assumptions we have reviewed can be the needs of teachers! In a study by Sharp and Green (1975), 'Mrs Lyons' sees her pupils as:

> the products of largely unstable and uncultured backgrounds, with parents who are, in various combinations, irresponsible, incompetent, illiterate, 'clueless', uninterested and unappreciative of education, and who, as a result, fail to prepare their children adequately for the experiences they will be offered in school.
> The parents, especially the mothers, tend to be spoken of very disparagingly. The mothers are perceived as generally immature and unable to cope, having too many young children either by accident or design whilst

13

they are still too young. The teacher declares that many mothers go to work to help pay off rent arrears and electricity bills incurred through bad management. She castigates them for creating latchkey children and for frittering away their conscience money on toys and unsuitable clothes in an attempt to relieve 'their guilt' at neglecting them.

'Mrs Lyons' is illustrating a rationalization often used by teachers: holding children's backgrounds to blame for low achievement in school. There are some situations where this may be true, but to see it as the end of the matter is to condemn children to the constraints of their backgrounds. And of course it may well be that some of the factors listed by 'Mrs Lyons' do not exist at all or, if they do, are not constraints!

At the heart of the issues raised in this chapter there is one issue: should education really make a significant difference to the experience of child, parent and teacher? Or should it simply transmit to each new generation the social distinctions of class, gender and race? Should it in fact be simply a process of social and cultural reproduction as Bourdieu (1973) has described? The contention of this chapter is that it should not and need not be; but unless teachers are constantly vigilant it will be. It is facile, misleading and generally untrue to say that middle-class parents value education more than working-class parents, to say that the education of boys is seen to matter more than that of girls, or to say that black parents have lower understanding and expectation of education than white parents. On close examination, these assumptions turn out to be false; most of the evidence suggests that the differences are non-existent.

If education is to provide real equality of opportunity then all the understandings and misunderstandings we have listed in this chapter, and many more to which subsequent chapters draw attention, have to be re-examined. Such re-examination can best be begun in the classroom. To do it we need awareness of social and cultural background and a willingness not just to recognize but to understand and value alternative forms of knowledge, language and culture so that we can base the work of the classroom upon a positive analysis of all children.

SUMMARY

This chapter has examined the role of the teacher in class, race and gender socialization and indicated the crucial need to break through stereotypes of class, gender and race. If teachers cannot lead in this then many children have little hope of real achievement. If teachers succeed then they will have made education matter – identifying feasible and rewarding achievements for each child, and delivering them.

REFERENCES

Bernstein, B. (1961) Social class and linguistic developments, in Floud, J., Halsey, A.A. and Anderson, C.A. (eds) *Education and Society*. Glencoe, Illinois: Free Press.

Bourdieu, P. (1973) Cultural reproduction and social reproduction, in Brown, R. (ed.) *Knowledge, Education and Cultural Change*. London: Tavistock.

Brandis, W. and Henderson, D. (1974) *Social Class, Language and Communication*. London: Routledge & Kegan Paul.

Delamont, S. (1986) *Sex Roles and the School*. London: Methuen.

Douglas, J.W.B. (1964) *The Home and the School*. London: Mac-Gibbon & Kee.

Eggleston, J. and Sadler, S. (1988) *The Participation of Ethnic Minority Pupils in TVEI*. Sheffield: The Training Agency.

Eggleston, J., Dunn, D. and Angali, M. (1986) *Education for Some*. Stoke-on-Trent: Trentham Books.

Jackson, B. and Marsden, D. (1960) *Education and the Working Class*. London: Routledge & Kegan Paul.

Labov, W. (1969) The logic of non-standard English, in Atlatis, J. (ed.) *School of Languages and Linguistics Monograph*, Series no. 22. Washington, DC: Georgetown University Press.

Mortimore, P. *et al.* (1987) *School Matters: The Junior Years*. London: Open Books.

Patrick, J. (1973) *A Glasgow Gang Observed*. London: Eyre Methuen.

Reid, I. (1988) *The Sociology of Education*. London: Fontana.

Rutter, M. (1987) School effects on pupil progress, *Child Development* **34**(1), pp. 1–9.

Sharp, R. and Green, A.G. (1975) *Education and Social Control*. London: Routledge & Kegan Paul.

Smith, D.J. and Tomlinson, S. (1989) *The School Effect*. London: Policy Studies Institute.

Troyna, B. and Hatcher, R. (1991) *Racial Incidents in Schools*. London: Routledge.

RECOMMENDED READING

Few recent books have studied the effects of social class in the classroom; research has concentrated instead mainly on the effects of gender and race. However, Ivan Reid, *The Sociology of Education* (London: Fontana, 1988) offers an up-to-date guide to the work that has been accumulated.

On gender socialization, Sara Delamont, *Sex Roles and the School* (London: Methuen, 1986) is an excellent account of the main issues.

On ethnic issues David Smith and Sally Tomlinson, *The School*

Effect (London: Policy Studies Institute, 1989) not only shows the ways in which race influences education but also the ways in which schools can overcome the negative aspects.

An interesting new primary school perspective on race is Barry Troyna and Richard Hatcher, *Racial Incidents in Schools* (London: Routledge, 1991).

Readers who wish to know more about the fundamental issues of socialization will find a full discussion in most introductory studies of sociology.

CHAPTER 3

Teachers and the curriculum

OVERVIEW

This chapter looks at the legally required National Curriculum and the purposes it serves. Going beyond basic, essential learning it identifies a range of tasks including socialization, social reproduction and selection and identifies the teacher's role in delivering them effectively.

> **Key teacher tasks**
> * Being aware of how the curriculum maintains social order and social control
> * Knowing how the curriculum helps to achieve social selection.
> * Understanding how the curriculum legitimates social structure and social selection.
> * Being aware of the effects of the 'hidden curriculum'.

The basic curriculum in England and Wales is now prescribed in law: the ten core and foundation subjects of the National Curriculum plus religious education. Detailed guidance on planning the whole curriculum framework is provided by the National Curriculum Council. In addition to these prescribed subjects the Education Reform Act requires that the curriculum should promote the spiritual, moral, cultural, mental and physical development of pupils and prepare them for the opportunities, responsibilities and experiences of adult life. Schools are obliged to take these aims into account when reviewing their provision and revising it to include National Curriculum requirements as they change and develop.

This array of detailed requirements leads many teachers to believe that they have little control over the curriculum – that it is 'given' to them to teach rather than 'made' by them. Certainly the introduction of the National Curriculum in England and Wales and other curricula imposed in many parts of North America, Australia and South Africa reinforces such views. Yet the interpretation of the curriculum is still strongly determined by individual teachers, as ministerial speeches increasingly recognize. And even more importantly, the crucial decisions about which children have access to different curricula, what subjects at which levels, and which examinations they should attempt are very largely made by teachers (Gipps, 1990). And when we add to these considerations of the formal curriculum the powerful effects of the hidden curriculum, which we shall discuss in more detail in Chapter 4, it is clear that teachers have a major if not a dominant role in determining the curriculum and its outcomes.

This has been strongly reaffirmed by many studies: for example, by a major project on technology education funded by the Evaluation and Monitoring Group of the School Examinations and Assessment Council (SEAC) (Kimbell *et al.*, 1991), which shows that the ways in which teachers devise and present curriculum are a crucial determinant of children's achievement. Yet how they exercise this role is a more obscure matter that much of this chapter will aim to clarify.

SOCIALIZATION AND THE CURRICULUM

Why is there a curriculum at all? In more static, predominantly agrarian societies all the learning needed to achieve full adult roles and status could be learned through the process of informal education. Parents, families and communities taught the skills of farming, hunting, childrearing, manufacture and defence. For a tiny elite only, formal education in church and home provided the education needed for their children to follow professional, ecclesiastical and political roles. But the gradual advent of industrialization throughout the world eventually made it necessary for all adults to have learning that informal education could not provide. Workers had to be able to read the instructions embossed on the machines, to calculate gear ratios, to sign contracts and to understand their pay packets. Schooling for all became essential. Eventually in all countries the state took responsibility for building schools and employing teachers to provide and deliver the requisite new learning.

Initially the basic skills of literacy and numeracy were all that was needed for the masses. Meanwhile, the increase of private fee-paying schools (in Britain sometimes confusingly called public schools) delivered an extended curriculum, based on the old elite professional model, for the sons (and a very few of the daughters) of the burgeoning numbers of factory owners, managers and civil servants.

In Britain the minimum school leaving age has risen from 11 at the outset of compulsory education in the 1870s to 16 in the 1970s. Meanwhile, the age participation rate in post-compulsory schooling has, by 1990, reached 20 per cent at age 18, a figure that still falls far short of that in France (50 per cent), Belgium (80 per cent), Spain (45 per cent) (Pearson *et al.*, 1990). It is not difficult to relate the expanding range of subjects and lengths of experience in the curriculum to the changing requirements of modern technological society.

Already it is possible to see clearly how the curriculum became an instrument of socialization for the new industrial and technological society and continued to do so as new subjects were added in the nineteenth and twentieth centuries: science in the 1890s, technology for all in the 1990s. There are now ten subjects – three core and seven other foundation subjects – in the National Curriculum in England and Wales, each with specified profile components (defined key aspects), graded attainment targets for the four key stages (age bands) and programmes of study to ensure delivery. There is also a range of optional and cross-curricular topics. (Other books in this series go into the detail of the National Curriculum.)

But the curriculum, school and post-school, is not just an instrument of socialization: it is one of differential socialization. As our discussion of the concept in Chapter 2 made clear, education consists not only in preparing young people to be adults in the same society, it consists in preparing them to be different adults with differing roles, status and power. Education systems have always offered differentiated curriculum tracks to achieve these differences: state or private school, comprehensive or grammar school, college or university. Differentiated curriculum tracks also occur within schools: teachers determine what subjects at which levels different children may experience. This may be done formally by setting or streaming, but even in the mixed-ability primary school class children at different tables will be working at different speeds and at different work cards or books. Every child in the classroom will be able to make a clear assessment of which is the 'top' and the 'bottom' table, even though the teacher may be unwilling to do so. Yet, again as we have seen, these groupings may have as much to do with expectations based on aspects of class, gender and race as they have with basic ability. In this fundamental way curriculum is determining achievement and to a great extent life chances, and it is the *teacher* who is the operator of the system.

The teacher's role may be given greater significance by the National Curriculum. Not only do teachers determine the levels at which different children undertake the standard assessment tasks (SATs) but also, in Key Stage 4 (ages 13–16), they may also have freedom to concentrate on a restricted range of more academic (high-status) core and foundation subjects for pupils who are likely to achieve examination success in these prestigious areas. The status hierarchy of subjects is clearly demonstrated by National Curriculum regulations, the core subjects of mathematics, English, science being more important (and the only subjects assessed in Key Stage 1) than, say, modern languages and technology. History, geography, physical education, art and music may be placed at the end of the list because of the possibility of their abandonment by some of the most able pupils in Key Stage 4 and their non-assessment at Key Stage 1.

SOCIAL CONTROL AND THE CURRICULUM

There is yet another aspect of the curriculum that is vital to socialization, and to which all teachers devote considerable time and energy. It is the formal teaching of the norms and values required of adults. Originally this was wholly the responsibility of informal education – undertaken by family, community and workplace and augmented by the churches. In small settled communities such a system was wholly adequate: every member learned the simple norms of adult behaviour, was aware of the rewards and penalties that sustained them and was highly unlikely to be able to move to a different community with different norms. But industrialization brought geographical mobility, taking populations to areas with different or even no established norms of behaviour. Where there are no norms there is little social control. 'Normlessness' or *anomie* has been well discussed by Coleman (1968) in his account of the 'communities' of railway construction workers in the Pennines, where respect for property and life was minimal in an almost total absence of effective social control.

A first problem of the new nation states in Europe and North America was to ensure that communities lived by agreed norms of behaviour, of the state rather than of the superseded local communities. At first this was attempted by law and enforcement. The introduction of uniformed police in mid-nineteenth-century England and the sheriffs in the American West were two typical examples. Both were only incompletely successful, as a thousand detective stories and Westerns have demonstrated.

It was quickly realized that the way to achieve conformity was not only by state enforcement but also, as the earlier communities had done, by finding some way of *internalizing* agreed values. The churches were ahead of most state systems in realizing this and the schooling they provided aimed to internalize religion-oriented adult behavioural norms. Yet in all countries the state, which makes the main financial contribution to education, has required and still requires schools to deliver a range of secular values relating to citizenship and political and economic matters. The conflict between church and state education is now largely resolved, but recurs for example in present-day attempts to establish Muslim schools in Britain and interdenominational schools in Northern Ireland.

These issues have immense relevance to teaching, now as always. Let us consider some contemporary examples. We may begin with the story by Hanson (1973) of the Royal Wedding Project. In his satirical paper, Hanson drew attention to the way in which, at the time, many schools were running curriculum projects on the marriage of Princess Anne and Captain Mark Phillips. With tongue in cheek he made a number of outrageous suggestions as to how teachers could enhance their projects. But his discussion also drew attention to fundamental issues. The present writer's own experiences of subsequent royal events confirm that, without any official directive, very large numbers of teachers up and down the country spontaneously decide to undertake a project on these events and, what is more, appear to be doing so with remarkable similarity. Another and perhaps even more important feature is the way in which the projects transmit unambiguous messages on the social structure of contemporary Britain. The nature of the traditional wedding service and its implications and the role of the established church are emphasized. (Yet at least two of the lessons on these themes seen by the present writer were in fact being conducted by teachers who had asked, on moral grounds, to be excused from timetabled teaching of religious education.) Most discussions of the events emphasized the long-established position of the royal family in the social system and the relative positions of others. Children were shown that, at the ceremony, high-status people were occupying the front rows, lesser categories were further away from the central aisle. More significantly, children quickly came to realize that for the vast majority of people the best hope was to have a place to stand outside. Pupils were coming to recognize not only the status divisions of society but also that their place was in most cases on the street along the procession route.

Over the years there is little doubt that teachers have been highly effective in presenting such information. Acceptance of the social system – its institutions, divisions, behaviours and constraints and privileges – is almost total. But a Royal Wedding Project is but one example of the socialization process. As Hanson reminded us, the next stage in almost all schools would be the commencement of a Christmas Project.

Yet another example is to be seen in the account of 'Miss Sanders' and her response to 'Donnie', a boy with a broken arm. It is drawn from an advertisement for educational films in an American educational

21

technology magazine which starts with a picture of Donnie and continues:

> You're all hanging up your coats at school and in comes Donnie with a cast on his arm. Everybody has to see it and touch it and write on it. 'How long do you have to wear it, Donnie?' 'Miss Sanders, what makes bones?' 'How can you break your arm swimming?' 'Will it grow back, Miss Sanders?' This is the teachable moment. It's the rare moment when you really want to learn. But your curiosity sure isn't satisfied by seeing just the cast. You want to see inside. So somebody goes to the film library and brings back a film selection on bones. You put it in the projector and – wow – a great movie. This way Miss Sanders can teach you all kinds of things – more things than anyone would expect her to know – at the exact moment when you want to learn them. And it's alive, the way you're used to seeing it.

Miss Sanders, in this example, appears to be totally responsive to the immediate needs of her children and appears to have no thoughts of such weighty matters as differential socialization or social control. Yet it is a fairly safe prediction that her treatment of the incident with Donnie will be to embark upon a fairly conventional and supportive account of present systems for dealing with accidents. She will describe the hospital that treated Donnie and emphasize strongly the high-status professional role of the doctors who will have handled the fracture. She will probably also have mentioned the nurses, indicating, perhaps in subtle ways, that their status, though high, is somewhat less than that of the doctors. And of course she will have uttered socially reinforcing messages about the need for accident prevention and the areas of the social system where particular caution is needed.

CONSTRAINTS ON TEACHERS' CURRICULUM DECISIONS

But if Miss Sanders does by any chance espouse markedly radical approaches in her development of inquiry learning she is likely to find herself subject to a range of controls. Some of these may be 'external'. Professional, community and administrative pressures can effectively bring teachers into line. And every year there is a small trickle of press reports of teachers who are pressured into resignation because they have presented 'unacceptable' political views, or have encouraged children to be 'subversive'.

An example known to the writer was connected with a community service project in a school's catchment area. The senior pupils had a local reputation for indifferent or even anti-social behaviour. A young teacher undertook an impressive programme of socially approved activity with these pupils, whereby the boys and girls created and ran a playground, dug old people's gardens, painted their walls, cleared the local brook of debris and generally brought acceptable improvements to a rundown area. There was widespread social approval for the project; the pupils were widely praised. The civic leaders visited them; the local newspaper featured them. The teacher soon received promotion.

But events did not end there; the teacher and his pupils began to realize that the old people still had fundamental problems that could not be solved by direct action alone. They had difficulty in obtaining their rent rebate, and the local council was tardy in the repair of roofs and blocked drains and other maintenance of a kind that was beyond the children's scope. Teacher and pupils decided that some further action was needed and the children wrote to the local housing committee and to the local newspaper about the problems, urging immediate action.

The response was quite different in nature from that which they had enjoyed previously. This time the local paper was distinctly unenthusiastic about their 'interference' and redefined them as a group of teenage trouble-makers led by a 'radical' teacher. The coincidence that the chairman of the local housing committee was also a member of the local education committee may have had something to do with the difficulties experienced by the school. Certainly the teacher was encouraged not to continue with this particular line of action and the project was discontinued.

Here we have reached one of the fundamental truths: that the curriculum is about the distribution of power. The community service project offered previously powerless adolescents the chance to exercise power in society. In its first phase this presented no 'problem'; they were being given no more than the power to conform more effectively within the existing social system and to refrain from destructive activities. In the second phase they came to exercise a power to challenge some aspects of the existing system; in so doing they were, inevitably, challenging some of those who already held power in it. Not surprisingly this challenge was resisted; the existing holders of power in the community demonstrated the extent to which they were able to control the curriculum.

SOCIAL CONTROL IN THE CLASSROOM

We have painted a picture which shows some of the social control aspects of the curriculum. Occasionally these may be imposed on the teacher; more usually the social control comes from the teacher. Let us now consider in more detail the day-to-day exchanges of the classroom and study 'Miss Sanders' in action. She may begin with a clear awareness that her own authority and role are founded securely on the existing system: that to challenge the system is to challenge her own personal position. This too has its own consequences, as Keddie (1971) has made abundantly clear.

> For the teacher, social control may depend on his being able in the classroom to maintain publicly his definition of the situation. He may do this by attempting to render pupil definitions invalid. Thus he may treat pupils' complaints about the course with scepticism and subsume them under normal categories like: 'he's trying to get out of work', 'it's just a bit of "aggro" ', 'they'll try anything on'. These explanations may nor may not coincide with pupils' explanations of their motives. The general effect of teachers' explanations is to recognize the situation as conflictual, but to render invalid the particular point the pupil is making and thus to delineate the extent of pupils' rights. Equal rights are not granted to all pupils since the 'same' behaviour may have different meanings attributed to it, depending on the normal status of the pupil. In one C stream lesson a pupil asked the teacher:
>
> Pupil: This is geography, isn't it? Why don't we learn about where countries are and that?
> Teacher: This is socialization.
> Pupil: What's that? I'd rather do geography. . . . Netslik Eskimo – I don't know where that is.
> Teacher (ironically): After the lesson we'll go and get the atlas and I'll show you.
> A few days earlier I had asked this teacher whether any pupil had asked in class (as they had in some other classes): 'Why should we do social science?' and had had the reply:
> Teacher: No, but if I were asked by Cs I would try to sidestep it because it would be the same question as 'Why do anything? Why work?'
> Observer: What if you were asked by an A group?
> Teacher: Then I'd probably try to answer.

Here we see once again an example of teacher behaviour which differentiates curriculum according to different categories of pupil. The differentiation is ramified by the repeated interaction of teacher and pupils:

> Once pupils are placed in high-ability groups the wish to achieve at school in the school's terms is confirmed and situated in school activities, and is reinforced by their long-term vocational expectations. These are the pupils in the study who when asked about the humanities course in general terms show they tend to see it in the terms in which teachers define it. These pupils are more likely to move towards using the language of the subject as the teacher presents it, and, equally important, their behavioural style is more likely to seem to the teacher appropriate to the occasion, than the style of C pupils. Once pupils are accredited by streaming or some other device for a different kind of meaning and to be used to a different end from those of C pupils.

In the same article Keddie offers an example of how teachers reinforce social role expectations through the curriculum. In a lesson based on materials designed to show that traditional roles are cultural not biological, the following exchange took place:

> Teacher: No, [women] feel the same pain but they have a greater resistance to it.

Boy: What are they always crying for?
Teacher: Well that's temperament, isn't it? Anyway we're getting away from the point about the Eskimos, aren't we?

Here the teacher's definition of relevance eliminates a question that would appear to be perfectly relevant to the subject under investigation. Delamont (1976) offers a further example of teacher control of the curriculum situation:

Consider the following incident from a lesson on the history of the Napoleonic wars which followed material on British politicians of the period. As soon as the whole group had assembled:
Evelyn puts up her hand. Mrs Flodden acknowledges it, and asks what she wants.
Evelyn: I've got an epigram about Burke. Can I read it?
Mrs F says yes 'of course'. Evelyn reads her epigram and gets laughter from the class.
Mrs F gets Evelyn to write it on the board so anyone who chooses can copy it down. Then announces 'notes on the Napoleonic wars'.

This is an ordinary classroom exchange which, at first glance, has no features worthy of comment. However, it shows, as almost every other exchange shows, who really controls lesson content. As the lesson opens Evelyn makes a contribution relevant to the previous lesson. She offers an epigram. Note that by offering it, she implies she has no natural right to teach the class, she asks permission. (We can assume that, because Evelyn feels confident enough to offer her epigram, Mrs Flodden is likely to accept it – not all teachers receive such offers.) Mrs Flodden grants her the privilege – and then immediately 'colonises' it. She tells Evelyn to put the verse on the board, and so defines it as a piece of information that can be officially recorded. It is not, however, so important that writing it down is compulsory, as the notes on the Napoleonic Wars are. By implication, therefore, Mrs Flodden defines the epigram as marginal to history, the notes central.

In each of these examples the teachers are offering significant reinforcement of mainstream values, the existing social order and their children's place therein. The children are unlikely to try to enter St Paul's Cathedral during a royal wedding ceremony; they are likely to show appropriate respect for doctors and slightly less, but still considerable, respect for nurses. In short, they are likely to 'know their place'. Few teachers would readily see themselves as 'agents of social control' in this way, yet virtually all are.

But of course, curriculum learning of values and norms, like curriculum learning of knowledge and understanding, is differential. Children's school experience is related to the teachers' views of the prospective adult roles of the children and is designed to reinforce those views. Indeed it is through the curriculum that schools and teachers legitimate the differentiations so that children who begin primary school seeing themselves as equal will leave accepting that they are different.

All subjects can be used to legitimate differences. All children between the the ages of 5 and 16 study mathematics, usually each day.

Yet the proportion who achieve the mathematics levels expected for these ages is small (Schwarzenberger, 1988). What could be more just than that a few children who achieve highly in mathematics can have greater prospects than those who do not? After all, they have all had the same opportunity to 'make it'. The same argument can be used for most other curriculum subjects. Put another way, the experience of failure is as crucial as success to ensure the acceptance of the differentiated output of new adults for each new generation. The more sophisticated devices to measure achievement introduced following the Education Reform Act of 1988 are very likely to reinforce this process.

The selective role of teachers, predominantly delivered through the curriculum, has increased dramatically in the last two decades; educational achievement, measured by examinations, tests and end-of-school reports, has become the key determinant not only of starting roles, status and power in adult societies but also of finishing positions. It has become the key determinant not only of employment but also unemployment; in short, the determinant of life chances.

The picture we have drawn can appear compellingly neat: a state-determined and -assessed curriculum dividing and conditioning children to achieve a new generation of conforming yet flexible adults to ensure the maintenance and continuance of the society – all achieved with the help of willing, compliant teachers. This simplistic view has been presented by many writers; for example, Bowles and Gintis (1976) suggest that schooling is but a device for providing appropriately trained and conformist recruits for capitalist industry. Gleeson (1989) sees the Technical and Vocational Education Initiative (TVEI) in much the same way.

Yet as we have seen in this chapter, and will see again elsewhere in the book, the system is not simplistic. As Bourdieu (1973) has demonstrated, it is a sophisticated mechanism of social and cultural reproduction based at least in part upon a general unwillingness to overthrow it and risk the destabilizing consequences. More generally, it is welcomed because it does hold open the prospect of opportunity and social mobility – particularly in modern technological societies – in contrast to previous systems of ascription, caste and patronage, in which all but a few opportunities were determined by birth and could not be changed. Any injustice is almost certainly less than in any previous social system.

The most significant problem is not the system of social and cultural reproduction but rather, as we saw in Chapter 2, the ways in which opportunity can be distorted by perceptions of class, gender and race. Sometimes these can be crude and clearly oppressive. For example, a class teacher in an inner-city school, asked about guidance she was offering to the large numbers of Asian pupils, commented: 'The trouble with Asian girls in this school is that they all want to be doctors, lawyers and brain surgeons. The trouble is that this year one of them has actually made it' (quoted in Eggleston *et al.*, 1986). It is easy to be critical of such seemingly overt bias. Yet the teacher was caring and compassionate. She had an excellent reputation for obtaining 'ordinary' jobs in a difficult employment area. She wanted to offer the same opportunities to her Asian pupils and she did not want them to be hurt by over-ambition. But she had failed to notice their high ability, endeavour and parental support, and so failed to offer them the appropriate curriculum and guidance.

It is in these ways that the teacher's role in curriculum delivery remains formative, even crucial. It is only through an understanding of the significance of curriculum – its delivery, availability and recognition of achievement – that teachers can acknowledge their own importance and thereby make judegments which can be just and empowering rather than arbitrary and handicapping.

SUMMARY

This chapter has reviewed the complex purposes served by the curriculum and looked at these in the light of the contemporary introduction of a National Curriculum. It has shown that teachers, possibly more now than ever before, have a key role in the delivery of socialization, selection and social reproduction through the ways in which they make different parts of the curriculum available to different groups and at different levels. The chapter has tried to show that the more aware teachers are of this, the more just and sensitive they will be in their delivery of the curriculum, both formal and informal, visible and hidden.

REFERENCES

Bourdieu, P. (1973) Cultural reproduction and social reproduction, in Brown, W. (ed.) *Knowledge, Education and Cultural Change*. London: Tavistock.

Bowles, S. and Gintis, H. (1976) *Schooling in Capitalist America*. London: Routledge.

Coleman, J. (1968) *The Railway Navvies*. London: Hamish Hamilton.

Delamont, S. (1976) *Interaction in the Classroom*. London: Methuen.

Eggleston, J., Dunn, D. and Anjali, M. (1986) *Education for Some*. Stoke-on-Trent: Trentham Books.

Gipps, C. (1990) *Assessment: A Teacher's Guide to the Issues*. London: Hodder & Stoughton.

Gleeson, D. (ed.) (1989) *The Paradox of Training*. Milton Keynes: Open University Press.

Hanson, D. (1973) 'The Royal Wedding Project', *New Society*, 23 Oct. 1973.

Keddie, N. (1971) Classroom knowledge, in Young, M.F.D. (ed.) *Knowledge and Control*. London: Collier Macmillan.

Kimbell, R. *et al.* (1991) *Final Report on the Assessment of Performance in Technology*. London: School Examinations and Assessment Council.

Pearson, R. *et al.* (1990) *The European Labour Market Review: The Key Indicators*. London: Institute of Manpower Studies.

Schwarzenberger, R. (1988) *Targets for Mathematics in Primary Education*. Stoke-on-Trent: Trentham Books.

RECOMMENDED READING

It is essential that all teachers are fully aware of the National Curriculum requirements and guidance that relate to their pupil age groups and subject areas. The National Curriculum Council (NCC) regularly issues information to teachers – both details of legislative requirements and guidance – and is sent on publication to all schools and education libraries. Because the material is being regularly revised there is little point in listing titles: check for the most recent material at your school or library. At the time of writing, NCC Circular no. 6, *Whole Curriculum Planning*, is a good example of a short and very useful guide for teachers. Useful guidance, too, is provided by the *Times Educational Supplement: National Curriculum Update*, made up of teachers' reports and usually published in March and September. Also look out for information issued to parents; it is important for teachers to know what is likely to be expected of them.

The Equal Opportunities Commission (EOC) regularly publishes material on curricular issues for girls – look out for recent publications.

Alma Craft and Gillian Klein's *Agenda for Multicultural Teaching* (York: Longman, 1986) contains useful ideas on curriculum presentation for ethnic minority young people, as does Gillian Klein's book in this series, *Education Towards Race Equality*.

CHAPTER 4

Children's responses to teachers

OVERVIEW

This chapter helps teachers to understand what their pupils think and feel, how they influence the work of the classroom and how their perspectives can enhance the role of the teacher. 'Good pupil' and 'negative pupil' roles are contrasted and the crucial part played by the 'hidden curriculum' is considered.

Key teacher tasks

- Being sensitive to how children are reacting to their teaching – the content, the presentation. Are they showing signs of boredom or excitement, or that the demands on them are too difficult or too easy?
- Knowing the messages being given to children about the teacher's wishes and expectations. What is the 'good pupil' role that the children believe teachers want? And are some children cultivating the opposite: the negative pupil role?
- Knowing what the hidden curriculum is and how it is affecting the behaviour of children and teachers.
- Knowing when and how the teacher's reactions, messages and the hidden curriculum may be changed.

Waller, in a seminal volume published in 1932, wrote that 'pupils are the material in which teachers are supposed to produce results'. But, he went on to comment, 'pupils are also human beings striving to produce their own results in their own way'.

If we are to consider the teacher's role fully we must pay attention to the most important partners, the children. What are their perceptions of teaching? How do they evaluate it? In what ways do they influence its development? Not only do they far outnumber

29

the teachers but also they are the future electors and politicians who will take the crucial decisions on the conditions in which teachers work in the future.

PERCEPTIONS AND ATTITUDES OF STUDENTS

Possibly one of the greatest weaknesses of teachers is their confidence about 'knowing what children think'. This author, for many years a classroom teacher, was once disillusioned by a four-year-old. One morning the postman brought a publisher's advertisement for yet another reprint of Winston Churchill's war memoirs. The cover portrayed an aggressive, dominant Churchill printed in black on a red background. The young child took one look and said, 'It's the headmaster'! Not only was the head of the local school quite unlike the picture, being young and 'permissive', but also the child had not yet been to school. Yet the perception of 'a headmaster' was already clearly formed by the messages already received from the media, the community and, in particular, from older children.

There is an extensive literature on the study of children's attitudes, much of it undertaken in the 1960s. One of the early attempts to learn the child's view of schooling was made by the American anthropologist, Jules Henry (1960), who studied the classroom much as an anthropologist would study a traditional society. In doing so he alerted us to the significance of children's attitudes to teachers ('crushes' or hates), to school subjects, to possible adult roles for themselves. The Opies' classic study *Lore and Language of Schoolchildren* (1959) also made the special nature of children's attitudes abundantly clear in its exploration of the complex, rich and highly ritualized life of young children.

Do young people have a separate culture from adults? Certainly many advertisers, producers of consumer goods and entertainment seem to think so and their commercial success suggests they may be correct. Certainly some of the perceptions of young people may well be negative or indifferent to schooling. Coleman (1961) is one of the most striking exponents of this view. He spoke of distinctive 'adolescent social systems', not only different from but also largely opposed to the adult world, and suggested that this separation springs largely from the increasing length of school life and the increasing breadth of school-based activities in modern society. As a result the adolescent is 'cut off' from the rest of society, forced inwards towards his own age group, living his whole social life with others of his own age. 'With his fellows he comes to constitute a small society, one that has most of its main interactions within itself and maintains only a few threads of connection with the outside adult society. . . . To put it simply, these young people speak a different language. What is more relevant to the present point, the language they speak is becoming more and more different.'

The strongly worded views of Coleman were challenged by other writers, who suggested that the dramatic contrasts in the behaviour of adults and adolescents may at times be superficial and not always related to fundamental differences in value systems. The regularity with which adolescents successfully adapt to membership of the adult community is cited as evidence for these views, which were usefully presented in an article entitled 'The myths of youth' (Jahoda and Warren, 1965).

Yet though the 'separateness' of the child's perception is visible in America and some other Western societies, evidence is available from these countries and others, such as Japan, which suggests that many young people are almost more in tune with the 'official' goals of the schools than the teachers themselves. Certainly a strong picture of 'convergence' rather than 'separateness' is to be seen in studies such as Kobayashi's *Society, Schools and Progress in Japan* (1976).

THE FORMAL AND INFORMAL INFLUENCE OF STUDENTS

There is now general agreement that children play a part in determining their schooling. Although in most schools they are still called pupils – a term which implies lower status – the increasing use of the label 'student' in many senior schools may be seen to mark a greater recognition of their participation. In a few countries such as Denmark such participation is enshrined in legislation.

But in most school systems, participation is far less explicit and formalized. In most, until the recent past, the opportunity for pupils to exercise influence was usually restricted to the incorporation of a small group of senior pupils into a lowly position in the power structure as monitors or prefects, where their task was to ensure that the teachers' decisions were reinforced and supported by a suitably limited range of disciplinary strategies. But apart from this, the role of the pupil was essentially a recipient one and children quickly came to realize that teachers' questions such as 'What shall we do today then?' were usually rhetorical and not to be taken too seriously.

But in many primary schools, theories of child-centred education have led to a situation in which children's expressed interests appear to be used to determine what the content of the curriculum should be. An Australian report (OECD, 1987) noted that: 'Over the last 20 years there has been a marked shifting of emphasis from the intellectual training of children to the development of the whole personality

31

and a new stress is being laid upon the development through self-activity and social experiences of the gifts and aptitudes that children possess.'

The child-centred approach is now less favoured by teachers and parents since it does not always ensure that key areas of basic learning have been effectively achieved. Yet in the new subject-based curricula that now dominate primary and secondary schools there are still important areas where children are required to be inventive, imaginative and creative, and even where childrens' interest and motivation is still dominant. It is important to remember that it still remains the teacher's task to identify these interests and also the needs of children according to professional criteria that cannot be utilized by the children themselves.

In secondary schools there is also evidence of pupil decision-making even within clearly defined subject areas. Project-type activities, including problem-solving approaches in the humanities, technology, literature and other subject areas, appear to take pupil influence somewhat further in that it is the student whose task it is to help identify the problems, find solutions and evaluate them. In theory the teacher may act as no more than one expert resource amongst many others that the pupil might call upon in a process of discovery, innovation and creative experience. Such an approach is embodied in a number of the National Curriculum requirements, for instance in technology, where students are required to identify design problems and devise and evaluate solutions.

COUNSELLING AND GUIDANCE

Many schools now offer students the opportunity of choosing from a range of option courses; they can follow a combination of subject areas in their field of interest. Often these have occupational connotations with which students may identify. Schools with such programmes usually have a school counsellor or other guidance support associated with them – a teacher with appropriate training who has the task of helping pupils to make curriculum decisions in the light of their abilities, prospects and interests, which he or she has helped them to identify.

In their most developed form, such arrangements may come very near to 'mobilizing' student influence. The careers guidance, using diagnostic and advisory skills in detailed discussions with, say, Key Stage 4 students, may well have established a comprehensive list of the curricular requirements of the students preparing for their fifth year of schooling. To what extent is this 'authoritative' list of requirements binding? Let us imagine that the list shows that there is a substantial demand for business studies with keyboard skills, accountancy and other applied activities, and that this arises in a school with a long tradition and a heavy investment in the teaching of classics and the arts. What is the outcome likely to be? Does the school invest its money in desktop machines and cancel its order for the new classics texts? In practice the answer varies, as might be expected, in accordance with teachers and the ideologies they hold. They range from a steadfast refusal to abandon 'true academic standards in favour of fashion' to a willingness to modify staffing appointment and deployment policies in a way that 'facilitates the needs of the students'. Here again is an example of the interplay of the power and influence of the teacher with that of the students.

In practice, many schools effect a compromise in which there are explicit and implicit restrictions on the choices available to students, both between options and within them. In such circumstances the counsellors may even find themselves with a role that is translated to one of 'selling' the school to the students, convincing them that what the school has available and is prepared to offer is right for them – a state of affairs that has been described by Circourell and Kituse (1963) in their celebrated account of the affairs of the 'Lakeshore' High School, where such practices not only occurred but were also clearly recognized by the students. And in Chapter 5, on assessment, we note that one of the key roles of the school is the occupational and social selection of students – and the important part that each teacher plays in this.

Does this mean, then, that student influence is based upon only slender foundations; that in many schools it is at most superficial and that students are fundamentally only free to conform to a situation that is predetermined?

THE GOOD PUPIL ROLE

Certainly for most children schooling means being asked to play the good pupil role. The traditional ingredients of the good pupil role are familiar. They include paying attention to the teacher, working hard, being committed to achieving the rewards offered by teachers for successful conformity, no copying or showing of work to other pupils other than in specifically authorized situations, the ability to give the right answer or at least to feel suitably dismayed when for whatever reason one is unable to do so. In demeanour the good pupil is interested, enthusiastic, responsive, polite, respectful and desirous of pleasing the teacher. As Sharp and Green (1975) emphasize, 'he will be characterized by his busyness'. Good pupils will be expected to develop according to norms appropriate for their age, sex and social position, and the learning of these norms forms an important part of basic education. Central to the view of the development of children is Piaget (1958), whose categorization of the stages of development through which all normal children will pass is part of the 'inner core' of knowledge transmitted to all those beginning their teaching in the basic education course.

But there are other, 'reflexive' views of the nature of development that emphasize not only diversity but also a relationship with the social context. The work of Bronfenbrenner (1970) indicates the strikingly different 'models' of childhood that are approved and endorsed in different societies. And there are, of course, within every school, variations in the definition of the 'good' role. But there is little doubt that most teachers of whatever persuasion will have in their minds something approaching the vision of Sand (1968), who described the ideal child 'sitting on the edge of his seat, his eyes shining'. It is important for pupils to behave in these ways; if they do not, teachers are unable to live up to their own conception of their roles.

In other chapters we have emphasized the importance of children's race and gender in their experience of schooling. These factors are of crucial importance in determining children's role in school too. Gillborn (1990) in his study of a large comprehensive school shows how the role of a group of Afro-Caribbean boys is very largely determined by the ethnic expectations of teachers and fellow pupils.

> Teachers' perspectives concerning the myth of an Afro-Caribbean challenge operated in such a way that any offence by an Afro-Caribbean pupil could be interpreted as indicative of a more general 'attitude' (an 'inner drive'). In the case of this Afro-Caribbean male clique, who rejoiced in both the ethnicity and the physical independence of its members, the processes were amplified until the school took very serious official action against the three in the form of suspensions and even an expulsion. As a result of these processes Wayne did not complete his secondary education in City Road Comprehensive and neither Barry nor Roger gained any pass grades in their external examination.

However Gillborn sees the consequences of Asian identity as being markedly different. He summarizes:

> Despite the generic label 'ethnic minority pupils', students of Afro-Caribbean and South Asian ethnic origins experience school in very different ways. In both cases the pupils' ethnicity influenced their choice of friends and their experience of teacher expectations, which often reflected 'racial' stereotypes. However, teacher stereotypes of Asian culture and traditions did not mean that all of their assumptions operated against the pupils' interests. In direct contrast to the Afro-Caribbean case, for example, staff tended to assume that Asians were well-disciplined, hard-working students who came from stable families where educational success was highly valued.
> The differences in teachers' expectations of Afro-Caribbean and South Asian pupils were such that the students responded to school in different ways. Asian pupils experienced school differently to white pupils (witness the acts of racial harassment), but their relationships with teachers

more closely mirrored those of their white, not their Afro-Caribbean, peers. Some South Asians, such as Arif, experienced very positive teacher-pupil relationships of a kind unknown to Afro-Caribbean pupils in the age-group.

As a group, Afro-Caribbean pupils faced negative teacher expectations which transcended individual judgements concerning their 'ability'. Wayne Johnson and Paul Dixon . . . , for example, were both judged to be 'able' pupils. Yet, neither experienced the positive teacher–pupil relationships which Arif enjoyed. Consequently, ethnicity and teacher stereotypes did not place Asian and Afro-Caribbean pupils in positions of equal disadvantage; in terms of their academic careers the Asian males in City Road experienced school in ways which resembled the careers of their white, rather than their Afro-Caribbean, peers. In examining the adaptations of Afro-Caribbean pupils, ethnicity was the central factor; teachers' ethnocentric judgements were the prime obstacle to be negotiated if the pupil hoped to succeed academically. In contrast, although their ethnicity was an important factor in their school experience, the Asian males seemed to follow academic careers which displayed some of the characteristics of differentiation and subcultural polarisation which were also apparent in the careers of white pupils of both sexes.

Whyte (1986), with equal clarity, spells out the ways in which gender expectations influence roles. In her study of science and technology classes she reports many examples of such expectations.

Teacher helping girl in the workshop says jokingly, 'I don't often get the chance to put my arms round a pretty girl.' The girl blushes.
(To girl giving good answer) 'You're beautiful, you!'
While rebuking the girls, the metalwork teacher adopts a softer more pleading tone of voice, 'Go and do what you're told' with a rising inflection at the end of the sentence. This contrasts with the monotone exclamation 'Stop it, lad!' directed towards boys, in a more abrupt and aggressive tone.
'Isn't she a neat writer!'
When girl asks why she has to wear safety goggles, teacher replies, 'You want to stay beautiful, don't you?'
These well-meant asides make children more conscious of gender, and incidentally, of the associated differential expectations that the teacher has for boys and girls: boys must be dealt with firmly, even aggressively: girls can be flirted with, to 'encourage' them along. Boys will be messy and careless, girls are 'neat writers'. The expectations quickly become self-fulfilling prophecies.

It is all too easy for teachers and pupils to perpetuate the unthinking perceptions of race and gender stereotypes that work to diminish and constrain the achievement of girls and ethnic minority students. This is not to say that perceptions of ethnic and gender differences are always wrong, but that they must never be accepted uncritically.

THE NEGATIVE PUPIL ROLE

As the preceding quotations have shown, schooling is not always of a kind to which all students may respond with enthusiasm. It may have the consequences of making many children realize their inadequacies, conveying to them the personal experience of failure. There are in fact two polar categories of pupil role in basic education, both of them familiar to all teachers. At the opposite end of the scale from the good pupil role is its corollary, the negative pupil role. Here the components are sharply different: those of boredom, frustration, a desire to impede the teacher's role, if not to make it impossible. To such students, staying on at school longer than is necessary is unthinkable; well before reaching the minimum statutory leaving age they have realized that, for them, the consequences of participating carry little or no reward.

These polar types of student role were documented in detail in a report on *Young School Leavers* (Schools Council, 1969) and many subsequent reports. The attitudes and responses to school of those who leave at minimum leaving age are shown to be markedly different from those who desire to continue their full-time schooling. Their choice and evaluation of subjects, their acceptance of the behavioural norms of their school, their perception of their future prospects and the relevance of schooling to them are all fundamentally different. Those who leave early see themselves as having experienced an education that has denied them the opportunity of significant participation or power in mainstream society.

The polarization has been diagnosed by Hargreaves (1967) in a study of 'Lumley' boys' school. He writes:

> Those with positive orientations towards the values of the school will tend over the four years to converge on the higher streams; and those with negative orientations will tend to converge on the lower streams. On every occasion that a boy is 'promoted' or 'demoted' on the basis of school examination, the greater becomes a concentration of the two opposing sub-cultures. . . . For boys in high streams life at school will be a pleasant and rewarding experience, since the school system confers status upon them. This status is derived from membership of a high stream, where boys are considered to be academically successful, and are granted privileges and responsibility in appointment as prefects and in their selection of school visits and holidays. The peer-group values reflect the status bestowed on such boys by the school in being consonant with teachers' values. Conformity to peer group and school values is thus consistent and rewarding. In the low streams boys are deprived of status, in that they are double failures by their lack of ability or motivation to obtain entry to a Grammar School or to a high stream in the Modern School. The school, as we have seen, accentuates this state of failure and deprivation. The boys have achieved virtually nothing. For boys in low streams conformity to teacher expectations gives little status. We can thus regard these low-stream boys as subject to status frustration, for not only are they unable to gain any sense of equality of worth in the eyes of the school, but their occupation aspirations for their future lives in society are seriously reduced in scope. . . . Demotion to the delinquencies subculture is unlikely to encourage a boy to strive towards academic goals, since the pressures within the peer group will confirm and reinforce the anti-academic attitudes which led to demotion, and the climate within the low streams will be far from conducive to academic

striving. In order to obtain promotion from a low stream, a boy must deviate from the dominant anti-academic values.

THE HIDDEN CURRICULUM

Is, then, the role of the student confined to playing either the good pupil role with varying degrees of enthusiasm or the negative pupil role with varying degrees of hostility? Such an analysis is still far too crude to explain the subtlety of the relationships between teacher and student through which the work of the classroom is negotiated. To take matters further we must look at the 'hidden' curriculum. Jackson (1968) in his *Life in Classrooms* (inspired by the earlier work of Henry) saw it as a:

> hidden curriculum which each student (and teacher) must master if he is to make his way satisfactorily through the school. The demands created by these features of classroom life may be contrasted with the academic demands – the 'official' curriculum, so to speak – to which educators have traditionally paid most attention. As might be expected, the two curriculums are related to each other in several important ways. . . . Indeed, many of the rewards and punishments that sound as if they are being dispensed on the basis of academic success and failure are really more closely related to the mastery of the hidden curriculum.

Jackson argues that every child and every teacher has to learn this essential curriculum if they are to survive in the classroom and even to begin to participate effectively in it. The concept is important not only for the revelation of previously unrecognized aspects of the classroom but also because it alerts us to previously unrecognized ways in which the student plays an important part, at times even the major part, in defining and evaluating classroom activity.

To recognize the hidden curriculum more clearly we may, with some assistance from Jackson, draw up a list of components that will be familiar to every reader with experience of school classrooms. It is, of course, impossible to compile a complete list but some of the central items will be:

1 Learning to 'live in crowds', involving the postponement or even the denial of personal desires, such as talking to a teacher who is already talking with somebody else; the ability to tolerate or to ignore interruption and disturbance; the capacity to wait an hour for the purple paint, or even a week for items such as the wood saw or drill because others are using them at a time when one urgently desires to use them oneself.

2 Learning to accept assessment by others, not only by teachers but also by fellow pupils. Lacey (1970) in his account of Hightown Grammar School makes this clear:

When I first started observing the first-year classes, the members of each class had been together for only about six months, but each class already had a definite structure of which pupils clearly had a detailed knowledge. When a master called a boy to read or answer a question, others could be seen giving each other significant looks which clearly indicated that they knew what to expect. On one occasion, for example, a master asked three boys to stay behind after the lesson to help him with a task calling for a sense of responsibility and co-operation. He called out 'Williams, Maun and Sherring'. The class burst into spontaneous laughter, and there were unbelieving cries of 'What! Sherring?' The master corrected himself. 'No, not Sherring, Shadwell.' From the context of the incident it was clear that Sherring's reputation was already inconsistent with the qualities expected of a monitor.

3 Learning how to compete to please both teachers and fellow students and obtain their praise, reward and esteem by appropriate behaviours. This also involves attracting attention to these behaviours and on occasions a capacity to forgo the rewards for other desired personal advantages. As Henry (1960) puts it, 'What the child learns is how to give an acceptable performance'. Every child in every schoolroom has to know how to give teachers what they want, every teacher has to frame wants that are not only feasible and satisfying to students but which also embody sufficient clues for children to be able to identify clearly what is wanted.

4 Learning how to be differentiated. Jackson (1968) draws attention to this part of the curriculum:

> the fact of unequal power is a feature of classroom life to which students must become accustomed. The difference in authority between the teacher and his students is related, quite obviously, to the evaluative aspects of classroom life. But it involves much more than the distribution of praise and reproof. This difference provides the most salient feature of the social structure of the classroom and its consequences relate to the broader conditions of freedom, privilege, and responsibility, as manifest in classroom affairs.

Developing a capacity to live with and to tolerate social differentiation is a key consequence of the hidden curriculum. It is well known that in most school systems students may complain with some bitterness about the injustices of their fellows who hold higher-status roles, such as 'prefect' or 'captain' or 'monitor'. Yet rarely, if at all, do they complain about the existence of such roles; the hidden curriculum has taught them to accept this. Students come to have a clear view of the social structure and of their own position in it and frequently differentiate themselves sharply from their fellows in different positions with remarks such as 'I wouldn't join that stuck-up bunch' or conversely 'I couldn't bear going with that group of punks'. In this way the hidden curriculum plays an important part in both the choice of social roles and relationships and their acceptability.

5   Learning ways to control the speed and progress of what the teacher presents in the official curriculum. Classrooms abound with skilful devices where, through distracting teachers with diversionary questioning, bogus claims that familiar material is in fact unfamiliar and difficult, the losing of pens and pencils and a thousand other delaying strategies, students are able to exercise substantial control over the speed with which they are required to work and learn.

But as Dreeben (1967) has made clear, the underlying purpose of the hidden curriculum, as with the official curriculum, is to learn the norms that are of relevance to society. He writes:

> Four norms have particular relevance to economic and political participation in industrial societies: those of independence, achievement, universalism, and specificity. I have selected these, not because they form an exhaustive list, but because they are central to the dominant, non-familiar activities of adults in American society. In school, pupils participate in activities where they are expected to act as if they were conforming to these norms whether they actually accept them at a particular time or not. Through such participation, it is my belief, pupils will in time know their content, accept them as binding upon themselves, and act in accordance with them in appropriate situations.

For the child at school, learning the hidden curriculum becomes an urgent necessity, preceding any hope of effective participation in the official curriculum. Where to sit and how? What fine balance of attention or indifference is tolerable both to the teacher and to classmates? How fully to respond to the teacher's questioning? With what vocabulary and what intonation to talk to the teacher? Which fellow pupils and teachers must be respected and tolerated, which must be distrusted and not tolerated? The hidden curriculum, like the official curriculum, is vast, detailed and complex. But unlike the official curriculum the sanctions that enforce it are usually inexorable and virtually inescapable. Much the same may be said for the new teachers. They too have to be keenly sensitive, as Geer (1968) reminds us:

> By listening carefully to what a teacher says he wants in class and comparing among themselves what grades or comments he gives for what kinds of work, and by 'trying things on' . . . in the early days of a school term, a class may reach a consensus about a teacher's standards, both academic and disciplinary. It then transforms what the teacher says and does into rules for him to follow. He must not change the rules the class makes for him, and he must apply them to all pupils.

WHY THE HIDDEN CURRICULUM IS IMPORTANT

Certainly the hidden curriculum is essential learning for both student and teacher. Without it the working of the official curriculum would collapse. Consider, for instance, the work of the mathematics teacher who in the official curriculum will often emphasize the importance of individual work and the negative aspects of cheating or other collaborative activities when students are called upon to solve problems. Yet every teacher of mathematics knows that student collaboration to find the correct answers is widespread and that, were this not the case, the quantity of wrong answers that would have to be corrected would be so vast that marking and assessment would almost certainly break down. Cheating and collaboration are essential if the official curriculum is to continue. Occasionally the teacher may recognize the dissonance that is mutually tolerated by telling a child who has been caught in particularly flagrant circumstances, 'You shouldn't have been so stupid as to get caught.'

In some circumstances the hidden curriculum is used for almost explicit negotiation between teachers and taught. At Wabash High School, well known in sociological literature, the school administration was seen to have a keen desire for a well-ordered institution yet did not impose close supervision of the grading system. In consequence there developed, through the hidden curriculum, a well-worked-out 'trading system' whereby teachers and pupils traded good grades for orderly performance. Rist (1970), in his study of ghetto schools, drew attention to the sophisticated collusion between the undemanding regime of teachers that allowed students to get by with low performance in return for which the students did not challenge the teacher's low profile of expectation. The National Curriculum and the standard assessment tasks are in part an attempt to eliminate such practices – certainly they are likely to expose them.

The hidden curriculum not only facilitates agreed 'production strategies', it protects both teachers and students from excessive demands on each other. In short, it facilitates and contains the official order by establishing the 'dialectic' of the classroom. Again, Jackson (1968) reminds us:

> Consider as an instance, the common teaching practice of giving a student credit for trying. What do teachers mean when they say a student tries to do his work? They mean, in essence, that he complies with the procedural expectations of the institution. He does his homework (though incorrectly), he raises his hand during class discussion (though he doesn't turn the page very often). He is, in other words, a 'model' student, though not necessarily a good one.

The hidden curriculum has been discussed at length because it is through the hidden curriculum, above all, that the powerful influence of children on the practices of the classroom occurs, an influence that determines much of the role of the teacher. It is an essential feature in the maintenance of order and control in the classroom and every teacher must learn it and be sensitive to it. But it also constitutes

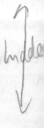

the most permanent learning of schooling. For most adults most of the official curriculum is ephemeral, soon to be forgotten in all but the most generalized recollections. But the learnings of the hidden curriculum endure, for they constitute the rules of living with one's fellows. For this reason they dominate the remembered experience of teaching and so exercise a disproportionate influence on adult perceptions of teachers. There is abundant evidence that politicians are regularly guided by such recollections – as are employers and parents.

For many reasons this is incompletely recognized in most schools. As a result there often appears to be a contrast between public expectations and school practice. In modern democratic societies the traditional 'authority' roles of teachers are seen to fit uneasily. For instance, the support for child-centred approaches in the early years of compulsory education seems to contrast with the regimes that appear to dominate many schools. Teachers, faced with demands that seem to conflict with the traditional expectations of their professional role, experience unease and difficulty and may even feel themselves to be failures – unable to respond to apparently irreconcilable demands for spontaneity and order, for creativity and high standards, for independence and co-operation. The imposition of national curricula in England and Wales and elsewhere sharpens this conflict.

Yet such conflicts, it is argued, are more apparent than real. We may perceive the reality if we can come to see the very strong and active influence of the child more clearly. It is the child's 'hidden' input that reconciles the conflicts and makes the 'impossible' tasks of the teachers and the schools possible. We often underestimate the extent to which children can live with and reconcile conflict. It is hoped that, as an important component of emergent policies on education, teachers can come to understand and recognize the child's true role more clearly and sensitively. To paraphrase Bernstein, 'if the perceptions of the teacher are to be in the mind of the child then first of all the perceptions of the child must be in the mind of the teacher'.

The final words of this chapter must, however, go to the contributions that children make to each other. Perhaps at all stages, and unquestionably in the early years, the most significant feature of schooling is that it allows children to learn from each other. Such learnings – of the skills of living together, co-operation and competition, sharing and dividing, determining and implementing collective and personal goals – can best be learnt from one's fellows.

The adult teacher may inspire and facilitate by example and management but the true teachers are the other children. If compulsory schooling did not exist we would almost certainly have had to create institutions in which children could mix and learn in our modern societies. Only by so doing could we ensure future generations of well adjusted and well prepared citizens.

SUMMARY

This chapter has reviewed the evidence on children's views of schooling and teaching and the ways in which these lead them to classroom roles which may enhance or impede the work of the teacher. In particular the significance of the hidden curriculum has been discussed. Unless teachers are fully aware of this then their understanding of classroom dynamics is seriously incomplete.

REFERENCES

Baratz, S.S. and Baratz, J.G. (1970) Early childhood intervention: the social science basis of institutionalized racism, *Harvard Education Review* **40**(2).

Bronfenbrenner, U. (1970) *Two Worlds of Childhoods: US and USSR*. New York: Russell Sage.

Circourell, A.V. and Kituse, J.I. (1963) *The Educational Decision Makers*. Indianapolis: Bobbs-Merrill.

Coleman, J. (1961) *The Adolescent Society*. Glencoe, Illinois: Free Press.

Dreeben, R. (1967) The contribution of schooling to the learning of norms, *Harvard Educational Review* **37**(21).

Geer, B. (1968) Teaching, in *International Encyclopedia of the Social Sciences*. New York: Free Press.

Gillborn, D. (1990) *'Race', Ethnicity and Education*. London: Unwin Hyman.

Hargreaves, D. (1967) *Social Relations in a Secondary School*. London: Routledge & Kegan Paul.

Henry, J. (1960) A cross-cultural outline of education, *Current Anthropology* **1**(4).

Jackson, P.W. (1968) *Life in Classrooms*. New York: Holt, Rinehart & Winston.

Jahoda, M. and Warren, N. (1965) The myth of youth, *Sociology of Education* **38**.

Kobayashi, T. (1976) *Society, Schools and Progress in Japan*. Oxford: Pergamon.

Lacey, C. (1970) *Hightown Grammar: The School as a Social System*. Manchester: Manchester University Press.

Opie, I. and Opie, P. (1959) *The Lore and Language of Schoolchildren*. Oxford: Oxford University Press.

Organisation for Economic Co-operation and Development (1987) *Country Report, Australia: SME/ET/78.88*. Paris: OECD.

Piaget, J. (1958) *The Development of Logical Thinking from Childhood to Adolescence*. London: Routledge & Kegan Paul.

Rist, R. (1970) Student social class and teacher expectation, *Harvard Educational Review* **40**(30).

Sand, O. (1968) reported in McClure, J.S. (ed.) *Curriculum Innovation in Practice*. London: HMSO.

Schools Council (1969) *Young School Leavers*. London: HMSO.

Sharp, R. and Green, A.G. (1975) *Education and Social Control*. London: Routledge & Kegan Paul.

Waller, W. (1932) *The Sociology of Teaching*. New York: Wiley.

Whyte, J. (1986) *Girls into Science and Technology*. London: Routledge.

RECOMMENDED READING

David Gillborn, *'Race', Ethnicity and Education* (London: Unwin Hyman, 1990) offers an illuminating account of how Afro-Caribbean boys and Asian boys have distinctive roles that are largely created in and by the school (Chs 1–4). Well worth reading despite the fact that girls attract little attention. Of course that is also significant!

Judith Whyte, *Girls into Science and Technology* (London: Routledge, 1986) is a fascinating study of how girls in fact get diverted from science and technology. Contains many breathtakingly sexist quotations from science and technology teachers.

Willard Waller, *The Sociology of Teaching* (New York: Wiley, 1932) is probably still the wisest book ever written about life in classrooms. Virtually unnoticed when it was published, it is now a classic. Dig it out from the far recesses of the library!

CHAPTER 5

The teacher as assessor

OVERVIEW

All teachers must assess children's work if they, their pupils and their pupils' parents are to know what achievement is taking place and build upon it effectively. This requirement is now being strongly emphasized by legislation in England and many other countries. This chapter breaks down the assessment role into five major components and analyses each one, stressing that assessment is only a means and never an end.

Key teacher tasks

- Evaluating the results of teaching after a lesson, a project, a course unit, a school term or any coherent section of work. This may be either through the work of standard assessment tasks or by the teacher's own linked or independent evaluation.
- Enabling children to assess their own progress to sharpen their sense of achievement.
- Diagnosing learning difficulties and creating opportunities for development through modifications of curriculum and methodology. Here the teacher is acting as an applied researcher.
- Being accountable, reporting achievement of the children to parents, employers and public using profiles, written reports, results of standard assessment tasks, examinations, etc.
- Using assessment to negotiate within the school and within the local management structure to influence decisions about resourcing, staffing and facilities so that they may be more keenly attuned to the learning needs of the classroom.

All teachers assess children. Without assessment it is impossible for teachers to judge the effectiveness of their teaching. Without assessment it is impossible for children to know how complete is their learning. Other volumes in this series will explore assessment techniques in detail, analyse their strengths and weaknesses and consider the ways in which they may be used effectively by teachers. In this chapter we are concerned with the underlying purposes and issues of assessment, the ways in which the contemporary teacher's role may be enhanced and extended by a fuller knowledge of the nature of assessment.

HISTORICAL CONSIDERATIONS

Ever since the initiation ceremonies of early societies there have always been arrangements for formally recognizing the capacity to perform important and responsible social roles and to exercise the associated social status and power. This has been particularly so in the professions and in apprenticeships to the skilled crafts. But the opportunity to attain such recognition was usually ascribed by social class. The task of examinations, where they existed, was to legitimate the incumbent in the role rather than to select.

It was only in the nineteenth century that the practice of competitive assessment with rewarding consequences for those who succeeded became widespread in the schools, thereby reinforcing, as Durkheim (1956) points out, the individualization that has become characteristic of industrial society, in stark contrast to most traditional societies.

In its modern form, as a component of mass education, school examinations and assessment are essentially a product of the nineteenth century and certainly one of the growth industries of the twentieth century. Without them the education systems of our day would almost certainly be fundamentally different: smaller, less structured, less integrated, less influential. Like curricula, assessment has been taken as given; to be reckoned with but not clearly to be seen as a socially determined phenomenon. Broadfoot (1979), in her pathfinding *Assessment, Schools and Society*, began to focus attention once again on the sociology of assessment. She argued that the institution of formal evaluation procedures in education occurred alongside the institution of mass education systems in industrial societies, and powerfully moulded the development of the system from the start. Gipps (1990) has followed this argument and shown the ways in which decisions made on new strategies of assessment influence the curriculum and education generally in specific, usually politically determined, directions. Richardson (1990), in his deeply moving book *Daring to Be a Teacher*, reaffirms this relationship.

THE OBJECTIVES OF ASSESSMENT

Though assessment is essential it is never an end: the objective is effective teaching and mastery learning. Every teacher must always remember that marks, success in attainment tasks and impressive examination results, though attractive, indicative and important, are not the main objective of teaching. Neither should gaining marks be the main motivation of children; if it is then motivation becomes extrinsic rather than intrinsic. Assessment, in other words, is either an integral part of the activity being tested or something external to it. Ultimately the goal must be for all children to develop a capacity for self-assessment and be aware of how fully their achievement reflects their effort, mastery and achieved capability. Such assessment is the mark of a true adult, and it is important that the teacher provides a clear example to follow. Self-assessment is of course a key component of the self-image and self-concept that teachers strive to help all their pupils to build so that they can be their 'own man' or 'own women' in adult life.

HOW TEACHERS ASSESS

We are already touching on major issues. They may be put simply:

- Who should be assessed?
- What should be assessed?
- What value should be placed on assessment?

The answers in a truly educational perspective are already clear: every student should be fairly assessed, everything that is within teaching and learning should be assessed and assessment should be valued as an indicator of progress, not as an end in itself.

Though this may seem obvious, it is often far from the case. In the past many children have been believed not to have been worthy of assessment and have finished ten years of schooling 'with nothing to show for it'. It is to be hoped that the 1988 Act will put an end to this particular injustice. Only some aspects of schooling, usually academic activities, have been assessed and a totally disproportionate value has been attached to formal examinations.

KEY ASSESSMENT TASKS

In the day-to-day tasks of the classroom, teachers will use assessment in the various ways enumerated on p. 44. There is a kind of self-evident logic about the strategies, yet in reality they are far from easy to implement. Let us consider each one in turn.

1. Evaluating the results of teaching. One of the familiar strategies is the 'hand-up session' in answer to teacher's questions. Yet consider the case of a recent scene observed by the author. In a very successful, lively science lesson the teacher paused to ask the class a question. From a sea of raised hands he picked Githanjali to answer. Her response was wholly correct. The teacher replied, 'Well done, Githanjali, that was a good answer but shall we see if we can say it in proper English?' After a long, stumbling and embarrassed interval the teacher got what he wanted. But next time Githanjali did not put her hand up. Had she done so, she would have been urged to lower it by her classmates, who did not want another boring interlude. It would not take long in this way to turn a responsive pupil with real potential in science into one who, lacking feedback from the teacher, becomes passive and indifferent. The teacher's positive and well-meant enthusiasm to help her with her English could well lead to a wholly unjustified negative assessment.

Teachers' proper concern with formal language can indeed be a major problem. We have seen how Labov's studies showed that many 'non-verbal' children in classrooms had been reduced to this condition by teachers. Out of school they were able to argue fluently, exchange ideas and make complex comparisons, but in 'non-standard' English that was unacceptable in the classroom. In consequence they were globally assessed as low- or non-achievers, with all the consequences that this entailed.

Examples are easy to find: for instance, there is the old story of the ex-pupil with low assessment in mathematics who goes into a betting shop and demonstrates his facility in calculating the odds, or in building his accumulator bet.

All these examples illustrate once again the operation of the self-fulfilling prophecy, whereby the pupils have come to achieve the expected. And, because their level of achievement has been 'confirmed' through testing and examination, the assessment appears to be wholly objective. In fact, as we have seen, it is often only a reflection and refraction of the teacher's own expectations and anticipations.

2. Enabling children to assess their own progress. Teachers are often content to allow children to identify their achievements by marks and grades. There is no doubt about the delight children obtain through achieving swimming awards, working through the Guide and Scout badge schemes, taking music tests and other graded procedures. Such incentives are important and not to be abandoned, yet they are only manifestations and need to be accompanied by an awareness of the real achievements that they represent as tests of learning, effort and performance. Here the standard assessment tasks can, if used as a means rather than as an end to classroom activity, offer real assistance. Certainly the spelling out of what each stage of attainment means is a significant breakthrough in identifying the elusive and unreliable criteria of progress that have often distorted learning in classrooms in the past.

But the problem about meaningful criteria is very similar to another problem familiar to teachers who identify their criteria clearly. Most children, particularly the very young, wish to impress teachers and to deliver what they believe teachers want. The author recently visited a number of art lessons in primary schools. At the first school he saw an impressive range of three-dimensional work on the Gulf war: the children seemed imaginative and creative. At the second school there was a very similar scene. At the third and fourth schools there was further repetition. It happened that all four teachers had been to an in-service course run by the local art adviser. All protested that they had been 'non-directive' in talking to the children. Yet the children had sensed what was in their teachers' minds – and had delivered.

Such examples show how hard it is for children fully to determine their own goals, and this realization has done much to lessen the high hopes of child-centred educational approaches of the 1960s and 1970s. But the difficulty must not diminish the attempt of the crucial self-assessment capability we sighted at the outset of this book.

3. Diagnosing learning difficulties. At its simplest level, testing shows whether children can understand, remember, replicate or otherwise achieve. If whatever is being tested is shown to exist sufficiently in all children, then learning difficulties can be assumed not to have existed (as long as the testing is being carried out fairly and on children motivated to respond fully to it).

It is important to recognize that there are distinct kinds of testing. One has little diagnostic use; the other can be very useful indeed. The distinction is between *normative* and *criterion-referenced* testing. A normative test yields only a rank order; it tells the teacher, and the children, who is best at an activity, who is worst – and all the other positions in between. Many tests are like this: spelling tests in the primary school, A levels in the secondary school. Such tests give little information about *what* has been achieved or how it has occurred. For this information we have to turn to criterion-referenced tests, which show exactly what achievement has occurred in the test situation, usually in detail. An easy way to explain the difference is to refer to athletics. A normative test would give one child as the winner of the high jump and place the others. Criterion-referenced testing would indicate the heights each child had jumped so that comparisons could be made, not only between children but with each child's previous performance.

Standard assessment tasks are criterion-referenced tests. These tests can be used to compare present with past achievement, so that even the least able children can experience a sense of progression rather than always being at the bottom, as in norm-referenced tests. However, the teacher must take care because it is all too easy for criterion-referenced tests to be used normatively – by children and parents – to judge schools and even teachers!

But where learning difficulties exist the actual diagnosis of achievement is difficult, and here the teacher needs to examine the failures and the incomplete responses of children, trying to tease out possible explanations, such as incomplete understanding, missing links in knowledge and faulty reasoning. It is vital that this is done *en route*; incomplete competence can often go underground, skilfully concealed by the child and yet undermining much of subsequent learning. Important work has been done in the field of mathematics on problems associated with learning about area (Foxman, 1982). The care and sophistication used by Foxman and his colleagues have led to impressive results, to be seen for example in the Cockcroft Report (1982). Much the same diagnostic analysis is adopted by Skemp (1989).

However, the main work on the development of criterion-referenced testing and the diagnostic potential of such tests in Britain has been the Assessment of Performance Unit (APU) of the DES (now the DFE), which ran from 1976 until its work was taken over by the School Examinations and Assessment Council (SEAC) in 1989. A key link between APU and SEAC was the Task Group on Assessment and Testing (TGAT), whose report (1988) outlined a way of combining external assessments of learning (which became SATs) and teacher assessment – both based on criterion referencing. The committee was chaired by Paul Black, Professor of Science Education at the University of London, who played a major role in the APU, particularly in developing testing in science, and one of the leading figures in the development of SATs for SEAC. Though the sophisticated diagnostic proposals of the TGAT report have been substantially superseded by changes in government policy and the practical problems of implementation they remain a major historical landmark.

The Task Group on Assessment and Testing (TGAT), responding to its terms of reference and the letter of guidance from the Secretary of State, stated that four purposes of information derived from assessments should be:

Formative: so that, the positive achievements of a pupil may be recognized and discussed and the appropriate next steps be planned;

Diagnostic: so that learning difficulties may be scrutinized and classified in order that appropriate remedial help and guidance can be provided;

Summative: to produce a systematic record of a pupil's overall achievement;

Evaluative: so that some aspects of the work of a school, and LEA or other discrete part of the educational service can be assessed and/or reported on.

The APU undertook major work in the sensitive assessment of children's performance in mathematics, English, Welsh, French, science and most recently in design and technology. Working in primary and secondary schools, it produced many reports not only on test results but also on ways of interpreting them in order to pinpoint children's learning difficulties. Teachers with specialist interest in any of the subjects studied by the APU should search out the relevant reports in their libraries: they offer a mine of good ideas for practice. Meanwhile much of the work of the APU continues within SEAC, which is responsible for the development of the standard assessment tasks in all National Curriculum subjects, and for a range of other tasks that include the oversight of the school-leaving examination, GCSE.

One of the most interesting ideas developed by the Assessment of Performance Unit was item banking, which, in a modified form, underlies the SATs. The technique was developed to ensure that whatever teachers teach can be tested and to avoid the normal practice whereby teachers teach what they know can be tested. The tests have to match the teaching rather than the teaching being shaped by the test.

To understand the technique, imagine a grid. The headings across the top of the columns indicate the aspects of a given subject being taught to a given age group. The horizontal rows represent levels of difficulty from the very simplest to the most complex (cf. the attainment targets in the National Curriculum). It is possible to put *items* in each box of this grid that children can undertake in each aspect of the subject at each level appropriate to their age. Armed with this *bank* of items the children can be tested on whatever is taught and no learning need go unrecognized.

The typical diagnostic approach of the APU was to present a task in a range of ways and identify key variables in determining different success rates. Foxman (1982), commenting on the APU tests, wrote: 'It is apparent that many errors consist of inappropriate applications of rules which are as systematic as those of standard or received mathematics.' But although teachers are well aware of the incidence of errors it is immensely difficult to predict them. Particularly useful illumination is to be found in the practical testing on area carried out by specially trained teachers (reported in the Third Secondary Report, pp. 14–15). This topic assessed pupils' performance in comparing the areas of three- and four-sided shapes and in measuring the area of a rectangle given a square unit. Pupils were also asked to estimate and then measure the area of an irregular shape.

First pupils were asked to find the area of two shapes, using a triangle as the unit of area. The instructions were as follows:

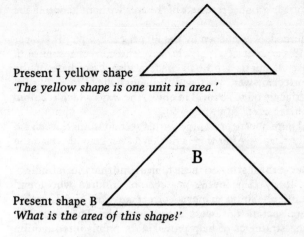

Present 1 yellow shape
'The yellow shape is one unit in area.'

Present shape B
'What is the area of this shape?'

The correct answer is 2 units, which can be demonstrated by plac-
ing the unit triangle on triangle B as indicated below.

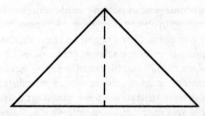

Some pupils placed the unit triangle on triangle B in one of the following ways and then estimated the area.

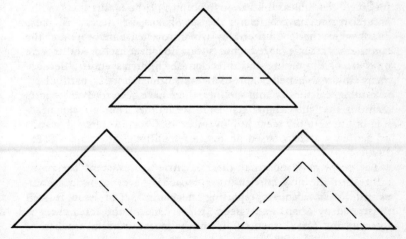

51

Other pupils made a visual estimate of the area without handling the shapes.

A range of methods was chosen by the 70 per cent of pupils (72 per cent of boys, 68 per cent of girls) who gave the correct response of 2 units. Almost all pupils who had made a visual estimate of the area gave the correct answer, whereas only about half of those who had fitted the unit triangle on to shape B in one of the ways which required an estimate were correct.

Unsuccessful pupils were presented with a second triangle as an aid in comparing the shapes. After this, a further 24 per cent obtained the correct answer.

The remainder of the testing on these topics confirmed such findings and indicated clearly that the 30 per cent of children who found visualization difficult could achieve correct answers if full rather than incomplete spatial aids were made available. This seems to indicate that the strategies of help provided for pupils often require a level of mathematical sophistication beyond that possessed by those for whom they are intended. More generally, it is an example of the need for *any* help to be appropriate to those for whom it is intended.

4. Being accountable and reporting achievement. For many years this has been a major problem for teachers. The differentiation and diversification of the curriculum began in the 1960s, the era of 'Curriculum Development'. Major national projects, such as the Schools Mathematics Project (SMP) and Nuffield Science, gave teachers a new wide range of subject matter and teaching schedule for most curriculum subjects. These initiatives were based on helping children to be creative and discover individual solutions rather than work through textbooks and predictable experiments, processes and exercises. Old, widely known norms of working through the established readers, basic spellings, the tables, the various volumes of the maths texts or the natural regions in geography, the set Shakespeare texts – all these dissolved so that the criteria by which parents, employers and the community at large judged schools were no longer useful. Adults were unaware of the nature and direction of children's efforts. Because many children seemed unable to meet traditional criteria, particularly in reading, calculation and spelling, there have been repeated reports claiming that educational standards are falling. Thus a major headline in the national press in November 1990 was 'Reading standards are falling' – a story based on tests of traditional attainment (TES, 1990).

The problem is not that there is little achievement to report, rather that the new curriculum approaches have not been accompanied by an adequate reporting mechanism. The issue is well illustrated by Sharp and Green (1975). One of the researchers is interviewing 'Mrs Carpenter', one of the most successful teachers of 'new maths' in her primary school, which is given the fictitious title of Mapledene.

> Mrs Carpenter had recently switched to 'new mathematics' after teaching a more traditional maths syllabus.
>
> 'When you've got a set plan . . . everything in its place . . . you taught length immediately after you taught so and so, and it was taught, you know, it was not a matter of children learning really, not the way we'd been thinking that they should be learning . . .
>
> Interviewer: How do you mean?
>
> Teacher: I mean we all, well, I have a little plan but I don't really . . . I just sort of, mmmm, try and work out what stages each child is at and take it from there.
>
> Interviewer: How do you do this? How does one notice what stage a child is at?
>
> Teacher: Oh we don't really know, you can only say the stage he isn't at really, because you know when a child doesn't know but you don't really know when he knows. Do you see what I mean? You can usually tell when they don't know (long pause). [There was a distraction in the interview at this point.] What was I talking about?
>
> Interviewer: Certain stages, knowing when they know –
>
> Teacher: – and when they don't know. But even so, you still don't know when they really don't (pause) you can't really say they don't know, can you? . . . That's why really that plan they wanted wouldn't have worked. I wouldn't have been able to stick to it, because you just don't . . . you know when they don't know, you don't know when they know.

Sharp and Green have diagnosed Mrs Carpenter as being in need of a 'reporting language'. It is through such detailed ethnographic studies of classrooms that it has been possible to make the case for more sophisticated systems for teacher accounting of the kind that have been built into the 1988 Education Reform Act and in much similar legislation elsewhere.

However, it is important for teachers to realize that, though mandatory and inescapable, standard assessment tasks are not enough. Even augmented by profiles, examination results and accreditation they can only report a small fraction of the totality of classroom development. Above all, they must be accompanied by the interpretation of the teacher, who can put results in context, identify progress, explain difficulties and indicate the ways in which parents can use the information creatively and to best effect. Fortunately this has been recognized in legislation and in detailed arrangements for teacher assessment (TA) that have been set out by SEAC. A series of *Guides to Teacher Assessment* have been published outlining sensitive and informative procedures that can be used for monitoring, assessing, recording and reporting (SEAC, 1990). However, the relative weight to be placed on SATs or TA has yet to be determined; it will be important for teachers to fight hard to ensure that TA becomes significant.

There is also a need for teachers to realize that, though there is far more to assessment than simply to implementing the mandatory requirements, those very mandatory requirements can put at risk some of the most important aspects of education. Gipps (1989) makes the point well:

> It looks as though, of the five characteristics of today's primary schools, two – mixed ability teaching and little overt competition – are likely to change in the wake of national curriculum assessment; two more – a variety of teaching and learning approaches and the integration of subjects into topic work – will not change *if* the SATs are able to encompass these approaches. As for the fifth – the easy informality between teacher and child – we shall have to wait and see whether national curriculum assessment has an effect on this.

SUMMARY

In this chapter we have explored the crucial aspect of the teacher's role as assessor – essential if the requirement to be accountable is to be achieved. Yet we have also emphasized that although apparently simple, and often presented as being so by journalists and politicians, school assessment is compex and full of hazards. To undertake their assessment roles fully, teachers need to be researchers: fair, objective, concerned, sensitive and interpretative. If they can achieve this they will not only illuminate the process of education for parents, employers and their pupils but they will have also acquired enough data to enable them to run their schools and classrooms with a new understanding. It is this management role which we shall turn to in Chapter 7.

REFERENCES

Broadfoot, P. (1979) *Assessment, Schools and Society*. London: Methuen.

Cockcroft Report (1982) *Mathematics Counts*. London: HMSO.

Durkheim, E. (1956) *Education and Society*. Glencoe, Illinois: Free Press.

Foxman, D. (1982) A pupil's view of Arithmetic, *APU Newsletter* 1.

Gipps, C. (1989) *Assessment in Schools*. London: Hodder & Stoughton.

Labov, W. (1969) The logic of non-standard English, in Alatis, J. (ed.) *School of Languages and Linguistics Monograph*, Series no. 22. Washington, DC: Georgetown University Press.

Richardson, R. (1990) *Daring to Be a Teacher*. Stoke-on-Trent: Trentham Books.

School Examinations and Assessment Council (1990) *A Guide to Teacher Assessment*, packs A, B and C. London: SEAC.

Sharp, R. and Green, A.G. (1975) *Education and Social Control*. London: Routledge & Kegan Paul.

Skemp, R. (1989) *Structured Activities for Primary Mathematics*, vols 1 and 2. London: Routledge.
TES (1990) Reading standards are falling, *Times Educational Supplement* (23 November).
'TGAT Report' (1988) *Task Group on Assessment and Testing: A Report*. London: HMSO.

RECOMMENDED READING

School Examinations and Assessment Council documents. These are being produced so frequently as standard assessment tasks are generated and revised, and political decisions are changed, that it would be pointless to list them as they exist at the time of writing this book. Check out the documents that relate to your subjects/age range in your library. A good start would be to read the most recent documents for parents: they are more readable and it is important to know what parents are told to look for. Much the same applies to National Curriculum Council documents; all schools should have full sets in the staff room.

Asssessment of Performance Unit documents. These too are too numerous to list individually. Choose from maths, science, English, modern language, Welsh, and design and technology. All subjects except design and technology have primary and secondary reports (design and technology secondary only). Maths, science and English were issued annually but also have summary reports for the period. All are a mine of information. Do not be put off by the dreary style of publication. Some have sound tape and visual material to accompany them – see that you get this too.

P. Broadfoot, *Schools, Assessment and Society* (London: Methuen, 1979) gets to grips with the underlying psychological and sociological issues. Slightly dated now but the fundamental issues do not change.

C. Gipps, *Assessment in Schools* (London: Hodder & Stoughton, 1989) is more recent than Broadfoot: it just manages to catch up with National Curriculum assessment. Already a standard text, and likely to be revised regularly. Make sure you read the most recent edition: the field is changing fast.

CHAPTER 6

Teaching about work

OVERVIEW

This chapter looks at yet another vital component of the teacher's role: preparing young people for employment. This task is strongly emphasized in the National Curriculum in England and Wales: the teaching of all subjects to all pupils between the ages of 5 and 16 should include making sure that children know about work and, in particular, the nature of enterprise. But teachers need to know about the nature of work in modern societies before they deliver these understandings. This chapter considers this and outlines some of the main contemporary approaches that are available to teachers.

Key teacher tasks

- Understanding the significance of employment, and unemployment, in modern society.
- Being aware of the changing nature of work with its concepts of enterprise, economic considerations and financial management.
- Recognizing that all subjects can and should help all children to share these understandings.
- Augmenting the curriculum with experience of the world of work where possible.
- Ensuring that all children are helped to identify adult work that will ensure the fullest and most satisfying use of their capability and are helped and motivated to achieve it.

For most students the end-product of schooling is employment, either immediately or after further training. It is a vital part of the teacher's role to prepare young people to enter work successfully at a level which matches their capability and with appropriate aspirations and commitments. For most adults work is the dominant feature of life, determining status, power, lifestyle and leisure. It commonly determines such things as place of residence and choice of marriage partner. In short, in modern society it usually determines social class and therefore becomes a major determinant of the educational experience of adults' own children. Following the 1988 Education Reform Act in England and Wales, with its strong emphasis on parent power and choice, this is a determinant that is likely to increase in significance.

In order to consider the vital role of the teacher in preparing young people for work we must spend a little time considering the ways in which work 'happens' in society.

Prior to large-scale industrialization the experience of work was indivisible from the experience of family, community and society. It is only during the past 150 years that paid employment, for most citizens, has been taken apart from the day-to-day life of family and community and transferred to separate institutions – factories, shops, offices, workshops and warehouses. (This is not to say, of course, that other forms of real work do not exist – notably in the home; see, for example, Pahl, 1984.) Such institutions are increasingly 'closed': for reasons of technology, security, privacy, hygiene or hazard they are accessible only to those who work in them and within their prescribed working hours.

Yet the twentieth century has witnessed a further development in the experience of paid employment. Not only is it a separable part of human experience but it is also one that is not being made available to all human beings. When twentieth-century societies first experienced mass unemployment it was believed that this was but a temporary phenomenon caused by short 'malfunctionings' of the economic mechanism such as depression or recession. Now it is realized that unless effective alternative strategies are identified and adopted, such 'malfunctioning' may become a recurring feature: unemployment has become structural in modern society. Many young people now have very limited prospects of paid employment. This is particularly true of special categories, such as people living in inner-city areas or members of minority ethnic groups. (For a detailed discussion of the employment opportunities of minority ethnic groups see Eggleston *et al.*, 1986.)

YOUNG PEOPLE AND PAID EMPLOYMENT

In this new situation major problems arise for young people and their teachers. Some problems are beyond the reach of any school 'remedy' and it is misleading and dangerous to imply otherwise. But some remedies have considerable relevance for the work of schools. One is that in many countries unemployment, especially for the young, co-exists with unfilled vacancies in areas of work that require skills, understandings and attributes not generally possessed by school-leavers. Thus there are shortages of young people for vacancies in the 'servicing trades' responsible for the maintenance of motor cars, television sets and other domestic appliances, building maintenance and other 'technical' occupations. There are also recurring shortages of candidates for higher-level work in computing, electronics and a range of scientific and creative occupations. One of the main arguments for the introduction of the National Curriculum with its emphases on enterprise education, technology, science and communication skills is to help to overcome these problems.

A second difficulty is that young people who leave school and do not find work often seem to find it increasingly difficult to obtain a job. Potential employers believe that some kind of atrophy develops: just as the muscles in a broken leg lose their power, so a total lack of work experience is believed to diminish the capacity to satisfy the very requirements of work such as industry, responsibility and punctuality.

A third, and perhaps the most fundamental, problem area is closely associated with the second: it is that work experience provides the basic contexts for 'normal' life. These include the use of time, the achievement of social 'standing' with its rights and duties, and many of the attitudes and values that underpin participation in all other social contexts. We may express the situation in two ways: (1) that vocational identity is the key to social identity; and (2) that work is the central instrument of social control in modern societies. Without the experience of work, how can the individual develop an adequate social identity and how can the society exercise the social control over its members necessary to achieve stability and continuity? The loss of a driving licence is a severe, even incapacitating, penalty for many people in paid employment; it may be of little consequence to an unemployed person who does not have legitimate access to the use of a motor car!

THE EXPERIENCE OF PAID EMPLOYMENT

We have now come to the crucial nature of employment. Like most human experiences, it has been taken for granted while its existence seemed assured. We see its importance more clearly when its availability is at risk.

Most young people see work as the key to the achievement of full masculinity or femininity. Willis's study of working-class boys in an

English comprehensive school in an inner-city area depicts the social pressures on the boys to take their place on the shop floor and so earn the acceptance of the community to which they belong (Willis, 1978). These boys need to prove themselves amongst their workmates as capable of facing and surviving the realities of the factory floor with its 'hard and brutalising' conditions. Willis writes:

> The lads are not choosing careers or particular jobs, they are committing themselves to a future of generalised labour. Most work – or the 'grafting' they accept they will face – is equilibrated by the overwhelming need for instant money, the assumption that all work is unpleasant and that what really matters is the potential particular work situations hold for self and particularly masculine expression, diversions and 'laffs' as learnt creatively in the counter-school culture. These things are quite separate from the intrinsic nature of any task. This view does not contradict, for the moment, the overwhelming feeling that work is something to look forward to . . . the lure of the prospect of money and cultural membership amongst 'real men' beckons very seductively as refracted through their own culture. (pp. 99–100)

Although Willis's study is concerned specifically with male roles, a number of other studies of girls and work identities indicate similar connections (for example, Davies, 1984).

As such studies clearly show, of even greater importance than specific occupational roles are the understandings and the self-image that individuals bring to roles. This identity is crucial to the way roles are modified and developed, and to the personal prospects within them. A label, such as machine operator, is but an incomplete guide to human behaviour in work; the identity with which the incumbents fill the role is the key component. How do individuals perceive themselves as machine operators? Have they chosen the work or is it a forced decision? If the former, what are the alternatives? Are these realistic or only based on fantasy? How do they adjust to the role in the absence of alternatives? What are the implications for other social behaviours? Fundamentally, is the vocational identity, with all its consequences, compatible with ego and self-image? Does it affect the individual's exercise of power?

The development of vocational identities is complex in modern society. In early, labour-intensive industrialization, when large numbers of workers were required to perform routine and repetitive tasks, individual identity seldom came to exercise a dominant influence on production. Their self-image was of relatively little consequence to most employers. Young people were fitted into their roles in conditions Durkheim described as 'mechanical solidarity': the role transcendent, the individual subordinate.

The concept of identity alerts us to an alternative process. It is one in which young people may 'contract in' to both the specific job and the labour market generally, rather than to accept them passively. This new approach is highly relevant to some aspects of contemporary social conditions. It is compatible with the expressed views of young people who wish to 'count for something' in society rather than to be 'on the receiving end' of 'the system'. But it is also appropriate for the needs of some sectors of modern industry, which call for human beings not to act as 'machines', but to use their capacity to adapt, adjust and initiate. For such occupational roles an active vocational identity is highly preferable to a passive vocational role. In Durkheim's terms this is a condition of 'organic solidarity'. For teachers this concept of opportunity is vital: it provides a goal they can offer to young people to encourage them to study, learn and achieve accreditation. Again the values of the National Curriculum strongly support this concept.

Unless an acceptable vocational identity can be achieved, then life for the individual is likely to be at best incomplete or compartmentalized; at worst, frustrating, enervating and incompatible.

THE ACHIEVEMENT OF WORK IDENTITY

As we have seen, until recently most vocational identities were acquired by predominantly informal means. The learning of occupational roles literally began in the cradle as the child saw parents at work in homes, farms and workshops. Learning was informal and vocational roles predictable for most young people, the circumstances of the parents determining the future role of the young and the learning appropriate to it. Such identities were strongly reinforced by the norms of the community which defined, often with great precision, such things as woman's work and man's work, noble work and base work. Definitions of this kind were sometimes strongly reinforced by initiation ceremonies as a prelude to entry to adult vocational roles, and these still feature in some apprenticeship schemes.

Informal mechanisms for achieving vocational identities are, however, not always appropriate in modern dynamic societies, in which occupational structures are changing rapidly, perhaps making it impossible for young people to be aware of the available roles in sufficient time to learn them and identify with them in anticipation. A characteristic problem of all advanced industrial societies is the rapid growth of new occupational groups, such as electronics engineers, television crews and advertising and sales personnel, which has meant that many young people enter work to undertake roles for which they have been able to achieve little or no preliminary identification. New generations of vocational identity regularly commence with each new initiative in technology and commerce.

SCHOOL AND VOCATIONAL IDENTITY

In the past half-century schools have come to exercise a major role in helping to identify talent through the examination and accreditation systems. There has, however, been little attempt to assist the young in achieving the identities to accompany the examination qualifications. There has been even less attempt to help those without examination qualifications to achieve such identities. This has led to many problems. Many young people have lacked not only an adequate identity for work but also for the other aspects of life that are linked to work. There has, for example, been remarkably little preparation for such activities as leadership in workers' unions. As a result, there are major problems in identifying leaders for these bodies at both local and regional level, with important consequences for the day-to-day running of our occupational and economic systems. Political and community identities also have seldom received the attention they deserve; potential leaders here too are often in short supply.

We have noted that a determining element in vocational identity has commonly been the social background of the young. Many writers have drawn attention to the small part played by schools in orienting young people for work. Becker (1963) suggested that school makes little impact other than to offer legitimation of the differences brought about by home and community. As Willis (1978, p. 1) says: 'The difficult thing to explain about how middle class kids get middle class jobs is why others let them. The difficult thing to explain about how working class kids get working class jobs is why they let themselves.'

Bourdieu (1972) sees this lack of impact as a consequence of the dominance of social and cultural reproduction processes that schools reinforce but do not change. Many writers, such as Lazerson (1971) and Bowles and Gintis (1976), have come to see the growing potential importance of schools as a transition institution into the labour force; an institution that 'accredits' young people with the various needs of the labour market (including unemployment) and achieves the necessary correspondence between supply and demand. Grubb and Lazerson (1981) demonstrate ways in which even new strategies of careers education have, in practice, been used to stratify the school system, and to separate working-class and ethnic minority youth from their white and middle-class peers by offering different work experience, expectations and accreditation.

PROVIDING WORK AWARENESS AND EXPERIENCE IN THE SCHOOLS

Some educators have believed that work experience is too important to leave to chance, or just be talked about in the schools. John Stuart

Mill, John Dewey and Kurt Hahn advocated this view strongly, and in different ways it is embodied in the curricula of the German Technical High Schools and the Russian Young Pioneers. In present conditions, when work experience cannot be relied upon 'just to happen' for the majority of young people, its provision becomes an urgent social need. In some countries it has become a major focus of national politics. Australia provides a typical example. In November 1979 the Commonwealth and States announced a series of initiatives known as the School-to-Work Transition Programme, $259 million being spent over five years on a range of technical courses, student counselling and special programmes for young people. The reason for the government's action was obvious. Already one young Australian in five was out of work, and another 50,000 were due to enter the labour market with little or no hope of a job.

Unquestionably present-day economic and social systems compel teachers in primary and secondary schools to take an active role in the achievement of work identity and the provision of experience in which it may occur. Watts (1981) writes:

> The world of work is central to our society, and to the generation and distribution of wealth within it. For schools to neglect the world of work behind rhetoric like 'concern for the whole person' – as though the role of worker was not an important *part* of the whole person – is abjectly to neglect a critical part of their educational responsibilities . . . the need for schools to address the world of work, but to do so in a critical and dynamic way, is all the more important because of the crisis that is taking place in relation to the place of work in our society.

Many schemes have been established to provide the understanding and experience of work in primary and secondary schools in the past decade. There are two main categories, which overlap. The first is known as *infusion*, whereby the subjects of the curriculum are regularly related to aspects of business, enterprise and employment. Infusion has become widespread in the teaching of most schools. Science has concerned itself with the practice of science in industry, mathematics with its commercial and business utilization, linguistics with careers in communication at all levels. In particular, work in design and technology has been closely linked with the experience of industrial production; indeed, the subject area has gone under the title of Industrial Arts in many countries. In all these activities, visits to industry and from industrialists form an important feature. The argument for such infusions is that preparation for work is not just another subject, it is what school is all about.

The current dominant concept in providing infusion for work is *enterprise*. The enterprise approach is based on a belief that only if young people understand how business works, how initiatives are taken, how risks are calculated and survival achieved will they be able to take an active rather than a passive role in their employment, so enhancing their opportunities and possibly becoming entrepreneurs themselves. Concepts such as risk capital, cost–benefit analysis, economies of scale, added value and the like become part of the dialogue of the classroom.

In the National Curriculum in England and Wales business and enterprise education is strongly emphasized as a key element in all foundation subjects, and in most cross-curricular themes. In its publication, *Curriculum Guidance 4: Economic and Industrial Understanding* (1989) the National Curriculum Council urged all schools to consider how and when to involve pupils in business and community enterprise. Education for enterprise, it stressed, means two things. Firstly, it means developing the qualities needed to be an 'enterprising' person, such as the ability to tackle problems, take initiatives, persevere, be flexible and work in teams. Secondly, and more specifically, it means taking part in small-scale business and community enterprise. Economic and industrial understanding, it is argued, requires both. *Enterprise Education in the National Curriculum: Agenda for the '90s* (National Curriculum Council, 1989) builds on this recommendation and signals the importance of both business and community enterprise. It illustrates how enterprise activities meet requirements in National Curriculum subjects; not only by developing knowledge, skills and understanding which relate to enterprise and are mentioned in statutory orders, but also by providing contexts through which foundation subjects can be taught. It shows links with the cross-curricular themes on which NCC issues guidance.

Nicholas Tate, Professional Officer, National Curriculum Council, writes of the publication: 'Enterprise education is already well established in all phases of schooling. It must now adapt itself to new conditions. If this publication is anything to go by, it should have few problems. Enterprise education deserves to be high on the agenda of all schools.'

A specific attempt to infuse work into the curriculum has been the Schools Curriculum Industry Project (SCIP). Jamieson and Lightfoot (1981), members of the project team, note that:

> the most common way of including teaching about work was by incorporating the topic into a course that already existed in the school for the fourth and/or fifth years. The majority of these courses are based round the theme of 'living in a modern industrial society'. Such courses are very often designed, or at least used, by schools to accommodate a variety of 'demands' made by those outside the school (for example, parents, industry, or the LEA) for the inclusion of subject matter which is thought to be necessary for a child's education, but which does not easily fit into an existing curriculum slot. Examples of these topics include health education, moral education, political education, economic education, occasionally careers education and 'the world of work'.

The authors are frank about the difficulties:

One can immediately see the potential difficulties of such courses. The treatment of each issues area is likely to be relatively superficial because of the large amount of ground to be covered. The course is likely to lack conceptual coherence, particularly if it is taught by teachers from a variety of subject backgrounds, which is commonly the case.

They draw particular attention to the problem that work experience tends to be offered more fully to precisely those children whose prospects in the labour market are most limited. In most secondary schools these are the 'non-examination' students. 'If there are omissions, then it is usually the top ability band which does not take the course, being left to concentrate on its examination courses.'

This exclusion is, of course, not inevitable, as Jamieson and Lightfoot recognize. But there are certainly difficulties.

The main source of the difficulty can be well illustrated by the case of pupil work experience, where the control of the experience which is to be examined passes out of the hands of the teacher. It is difficult to examine what pupils have learned about work from work experience placements which have all been markedly different from one another.

Yet another initiative comes from the Mini-Enterprise in Schools Project (MESP), based at Warwick University. Here too the emphases are on infusion:

It is important that mini-enterprise activity should include projects which identify and meet social need. A balanced education in economic understanding should examine why, despite the apparent strengths of a free market, some needs remain unmet and why resources sometimes need to be directed to desirable social ends. . . . There is a growing recognition of the need for a policy on work-related matters and a progression of mini-enterprise activities. . . . Insufficient use was being made of mini-enterprise as a vehicle for the delivery of curricular subjects and cross-curricular emphases. The Design and Technology programmes of study and attainment targets and the related cross-curricular emphasis on economic and industrial understanding of the National Curriculum are but some of the emerging initiatives which, wisely interpreted, could provide this impetus and lead to the adoption of more coherent strategies.

SCIP and MESP were merged in 1989 and their combined range of services is helping schools and LEAs deliver a broad and balanced work-related dimension to the curriculum. SCIP/MESP is now the largest UK and European industry education organization. Its aims are now defined as:

1 To enable young people to participate effectively in a rapidly changing industrial society.
2 To enable young people to develop qualities of personal initiative and enterprise.
3 To develop and sustain quality partnerships between education, industry and the wider community.

4   To promote industrial and economic understanding in all key stages of the National Curriculum.
5   To promote an active, work-related dimension to the whole curriculum from 5 to 19.

SCIP/MESP brings industrialists together with teachers to develop curriculum activities. It has pioneered work experience, work shadowing, mini-enterprises, simulations, the work-related curriculum and other active learning approaches involving industry in schools.

The SCIP/MESP approach emphasizes:

1   Teachers developing the curriculum in partnership with industry.
2   The involvement of members of the local economic community in students' learning both in their places of work and in the classroom.
3   Students learning actively and through their experiences of industry.
4   Evaluation of practice and its dissemination.

One of the most long-standing developments in infusion has been the Technical and Vocational Education Initiative (TVEI), which since the early 1980s has offered special funding to deliver programmes oriented to vocational training to 14- to 18-year-old students in Britain. Here again enterprise education is crucial. The TVEI Unit of the Training Agency asserts:

> The development of enterprise in young people is a major objective of TVEI and central to its aim of ensuring that their education equips them for the demands of working life. Enterprise education can empower young people to realise their full potential and make them more able to meet the challenges of social, economic and technological evolution. Young people themselves benefit from the experience of enterprise across the curriculum and business, the community and education all benefit if young people are innovative, able to manage resources, make decisions, and not only formulate ideas but translate those ideas into action and follow them through to a conclusion.

The thrust of TVEI has been powerful. Using substantial government funding provided by the Department of Trade and Industry rather than the Department for Education it is now a feature of virtually all secondary schools and many colleges of further education. Similar schemes exist in many other countries.

Students chosen to follow a TVEI course follow a normal curriculum in most subjects. But in addition they follow subjects specifically oriented to technical and vocational studies, such as computer studies, business education, applied technology, photography and catering, and may take vocationally oriented rather than academic qualifications. It is a measure of the success of TVEI that such courses and examinations are now seen as the normal work of many secondary schools.

Inevitably much of the work of preparing students for work takes place in secondary schools as the end of compulsory schooling draws near. But a very large amount of work occurs in primary schools, for example the Primary Education and Industry Project based at Edge College of Higher Education. This project has produced materials for teachers of even the youngest children and demonstrated their effectiveness. A short account can be found in Waite (1984). And of course all the emphases on enterprise education in the National Curriculum are applicable equally to primary and secondary schools.

WORK EXPERIENCE COURSES

At the opposite end of the spectrum to infusion programmes are work experience programmes. These are perhaps one of the best established of the 'additive' solutions within schools, both primary and secondary. In such courses pupils visit one or more vocational locations where they have the opportunity, over a period, to mix with workers at a variety of levels and to learn something of the formal and the informal culture of the work-place – the ways in which life is experienced by those who work there. In some situations it is possible for pupils actually to experience work with its productive rhythms, its rewards and constraints, but unfortunately problems of union restrictions, insurance hazards and many other administrative difficulties generally restrict such opportunities to casual work and certain kinds of low-skilled occupations.

THE CHARACTERISTICS OF PROGRAMMES

All school programmes have three aims in common. The first is to increase the possibility of successful employment and to ensure a more effective linkage between the role of the student and the role of the worker and to facilitate the transition between school and work so that young people, their fellow workers, their employers, their families and their communities find the change smooth, not disruptive.

The second feature of all such projects is that they embody a knowledge content. All identify a body of understandings, skills, values and orientations that are valuable components of vocational identity. All too often, however, this knowledge content is largely, if not wholly, determined by the adult participants. Yet we are increasingly aware that the understandings of the young people themselves provide a crucial component of their vocational identity and that, unless these are taken into account in devising such programmes, it is likely that students' achievement will fall far short of their potential. The incomplete recognition of the important understandings of young people is clearly to be seen in the earlier quotation from Willis's work on p. 59.

Yet a third aspect of school-based schemes is the range of adult participants. Unquestionably, teachers must play an important, if not the central, part in their organization. Teachers who have previous experience in adult occupations other than teaching are likely to have a particularly valuable contribution to make (though much depends on the perceptions of work held by such teachers). But in addition to teachers, it is important that adults working in industry participate: it is even more important that these include people who are doing the jobs to which pupils are immediately aspiring. Only in this way is effective and acceptable communication likely to be achieved.

THE EVALUATION OF WORK PROGRAMMES

How may teachers evaluate the context of school-based work experience? How can we tell if the visit to the factory is more significant to the lives of the young than a visit to see the lions at the zoo?

THE EVALUATION OF THE CLIENTS

Overall, young people seem to enjoy the schemes; evidence in most available reports suggests that they are seen to be interesting, certainly less boring than other aspects of school. In some schools attendance during work programmes runs at a higher level than participation in 'normal' school.

Yet much of the evidence of informal evaluation by the young people themselves is unfavourable: 'You know all that work experience at school – well, it's just a waste of time.' 'A right send-up that school visit to the brick works – my mates there were splitting their sides at the things they told the teachers.' However, plenty of evidence of more perceptive appraisals by young people exists, displaying an acute awareness of the benefits as well as the problems of work experience programmes.

Gleeson and Mardle (1980) report 'Andy's' views, which illustrate a considerable capacity to discriminate between craft-level work and technician-level work, and between the prospects for each.

> I wouldn't get the same opportunities off a craft course would I? . . . Craft work is too limited . . . there aren't enough opportunities to do really skilled work. Nowadays, most craft jobs are boring . . . repetitive work on machinery . . . where you don't use your brain. I wouldn't do a craft course . . . if you do, you're stuck . . . you haven't got the same chances or choices, have you? You've only got to look around this place . . . Most of

the craft lads aren't interested in their work or college . . . they didn't do
so well at school to get on a technician's course . . . they're stuck . . . they
haven't got a future outside craft work. If I couldn't get a job as a technician
. . . or something like it . . . I certainly wouldn't take craft work.

It is also evident that a very great deal of the learning of young
people consists of the reaffirmations of established beliefs about the
nature of work. Delamont (1980), in a study of adolescent girls,
noticed the way in which girls' expectations of differentiation in
work were powerfully reinforced by their experiences of both work and
school. Far from such experiences leading a girl to enter a 'non-
feminine' occupation like engineering, they appeared more likely to
deter her.

Such evaluations, loose, imprecise and elusive as they are, are
the best guide we have to the achievements of work programmes.
Yet in this area of education, more than in any other, it is the client's
experience and appraisal of these programmes and the opportunity,
legitimation and accreditation they offer that will ultimately determine the size, nature and direction of future provision. In so doing,
they will largely determine whether programmes built in and after
school will mark the beginning of a new relationship between education and work in modern societies, possibly involving some aspects of
a 'youth guarantee', or merely involve an acceptance of the existing
structure, often offering only palliatives to non-achievers.

New British government initiatives in the White Paper *Education
and Training for the 21st Century* (1991), endorsed by the Prime
Minister in 1992, offer yet a further attempt to change the patterns of
perceptions and expectations of young people and their parents and
employers. This is by changing the structure of institutions and
qualifications so that 'vocational' courses will rank equally with
'academic' programmes and so widen the definition of success and
achievement. In so doing it is also hoped to mobilize the 'pool of
ability' of young people more fully, to the benefit of industry, society
and the young people themselves.

SUMMARY

**This chapter has outlined the nature of work in modern society
and the crucial role the school takes in selecting and preparing young
people for it. It has looked at the ways in which individual teachers
play their part and how in modern 'enterprise' cultures this is changing, requiring them to modify their curriculum and management in
order to respond.**

REFERENCES

Ball, C. and Ball, M. (1979) *Fit for Work!* London: Writers' and Readers' Publishing Co-operative.

Becker, H (1963) *Outsiders: Studies in the Sociology of Deviance.* New York: Free Press.

Bourdieu, P. (1972) Cultural reproduction and social reproduction, in Brown, R. (ed.) *Knowledge, Education and Cultural Change.* London: Tavistock.

Bowles, S. and Gintis, H. (1976) *Schooling in Capitalist America.* London: Routledge & Kegan Paul.

Davies, L. (1984) *Girls Growing Up.* London: Macmillan.

Delamont, S. (1980) *Sex Roles and the School.* London: Methuen.

Department of Industry (1980) *Industry/Education Liaison.* London: DOI, Industry/Education Unit.

Eggleston, J., Dunn, D. and Anjali, M. (1986) *Education for Some.* Stoke-on-Trent: Trentham Books.

Gleeson, D. and Mardle, G. D. (1980) *Further Education or Training! A Case Study in the Theory and Practice of Day Release Education.* London: Routledge & Kegan Paul.

Grubb, W.N. and Lazerson, M. (1981) Vocational solutions to youth problems, *Education Analysis* 3(2).

Her Majesty's Government (1991) *Education and Training for the 21st Century* (2 volumes). London: HMSO.

Her Majesty's Inspectorate (1989) *Mini-Enterprise in Schools: Some Aspects of Current Practice.* London: HMSO.

Ivison, V. (1979) Young Enterprise: a school–industry link, *Trends* 2.

Jamieson, I. and Lightfoot, M. (1981) Learning about work, *Education Analysis*, 3(2).

Lazerson, M. (1971) *Origins of the Urban School.* Cambridge, Massachusetts: Harvard University Press.

Manpower Services Commission (1981) *A New Training Initiative.* London: MSC.

Mini Enterprises to Schools Projects/School Curriculum/Industry Partnership (1991) *The Enterprising Classroom*, Parts 1 and 2. Coventry: MESP/SCIP.

National Curriculum Council (1989) *Curriculum Guidance 4: Economic and Industrial Understanding.* York: NCC.

National Curriculum Council (1989) *Enterprise Education in the National Curriculum: Agenda for the '90s.* York: NCC.

Pahl, R. (1984) *Divisions of Labour.* Oxford: Blackwell.

Ryrie, A.C. and Weir, A.D. (1978) *Getting a Trade.* London: Hodder & Stoughton (for the Scottish Council for Research in Education).

Waite, P. E. (1984) Industry and the primary curriculum, *Education 3–13*, 12(1).

Watts, A.G. (1981) Schools, work and youth: an introduction, *Education Analysis* 3(2).
Willis, P. (1978) *Learning to Labour*. London: Saxon House.

RECOMMENDED READING

For practical suggestions of activities for primary and secondary schools the literature published by the merged Schools Curriculum Industry Partnership and Mini Enterprise in Schools Project offer a good up-to-date guide. New materials are being produced regularly, check your library for the most recent documents.

The final report of the Working Group on Technology, *Design and Technology for Ages 5–16* (HMSO, 1989), which has largely passed into legislation for the National Curriculum, is a good example of how preparation for work can suffuse the whole curriculum. The topic is also considered fully in *Teaching Design and Technology* by John Eggleston (Buckingham: Open University Press, 1992). Also a useful read for any teacher who feels the need to know more about technology in school!

The *British Journal of Education and Work*, edited by Professor Ian Jamieson, almost always has good, practical and original articles on the links between education and work. Most education libraries stock it.

Education for Some by John Eggleston, David Dunn and Madhu Anjali (Stoke-on-Trent: Trentham Books, 1986) is a well-known study of the path from school to work of a large group of black and white adolescents. The introductory chapter on the theoretical basis of the study is one of the best, but least read, parts!

CHAPTER 7

The teacher as a manager

OVERVIEW

Schools are now, more than ever, being run as businesses. Each teacher is an important manager in a team that is generating a product, helping to market it and jointly responsible for the success and failure of the enterprise. This chapter analyses these new managerial roles, their opportunities and difficulties, and recognizes that all the long-standing requirements of sensitivity, perception and commitment are still in place. Without these the new legislative requirements can, at best, be only partially effective.

Key teacher tasks

- Playing a full role as a member of the school management team, delivering a sound education for all pupils, presenting it honestly and effectively to parents and community and sharing responsibility for the outcomes.
- Sharing in decision-making and implementation of whole school policies on curriculum, assessment, equality of opportunity, guidance and community relationships.
- Managing the classroom effectively, with sensitivity and perception so that the needs of all children are taken into account and injustice, favouritism and victimization do not occur.
- Ensuring that the children themselves, by their own understanding and behaviour, play an active part in ensuring achievement, tolerance and justice in the school.
- Participating in the running of school in-service training to enhance managerial and other teacher capabilities.

In most parts of the world basic schooling has developed as a state provision in much the same way as other state services – hospitals, railways, post offices, prisons and the like. Though they are generally responsive to the wishes of the electorate, such institutions have usually been the direct responsibility of ministers, local authorities or official bureaucracies in liaison with the professionals who work in them.

CLIENT-LED MANAGEMENT

However, major changes in the concept of management are taking place in many countries. It is now widely believed that schools, like other public institutions, should be directly responsible to their clients. In the case of the schools these are the parents and the communities they serve. A consequence of this is that much of the power to control the schools passes to elected school governors or managers and away from local authorities and even teachers.

This move in the schools is paralleled by similar changes to health, social services and public architecture, where, increasingly, professionals are losing their customary roles and being made subject to consumer control. Perhaps more generally it is a trend that reflects the growing enthusiasm for consumer-oriented ideologies that has been seen so spectacularly in events in Eastern Europe and many other parts of the world. In order to achieve it the consumers have to have financial power so that, if they prefer to be treated in hospital A rather than hospital B, then the more popular hospital A increases its income and hospital B loses. Hospitals, like other institutions, and businesses, have to compete successfully to survive. If competition does not exist it has to be created, even in telephone and postal services. There are plans even for privatized prisons to compete with state prisons. (In this case it is the judiciary and the police rather than the inmates who are seen as the 'clients'!)

LOCAL MANAGEMENT OF SCHOOLS

In Britain this movement has led to the local managemment of schools (LMS), which is now mandatory in England and Wales and has the most fundamental implications for teachers. Not only are they now directly accountable to local governing bodies but parents have a freedom (subject in the short run to the overall physical capacity of the schools) to send their children to schools of their choice. It is highly likely that parents will exercise this choice in the light of the published standard assessment task results of the school for the various subjects of the National Curriculum and also on their view of the resources, facilities and general ambiance of the school. And as at least 80 per cent of the funding of the schools is being allocated in accordance with the number of pupils on role then the capacity of schools to recruit children is crucial and must be a key management objective.

This objective may well lead to the diminution of certain patterns of spending for special needs, for example those relating to bilingual children or to children with physical handicaps. These are expensive needs to provide for, but may contribute very little to the recruitment strategies of the schools. Indeed, with some parents they may constitute a negative feature; these parents may see it as an indication that a school is preoccupied with 'problem' or 'difficult' children rather than mainstream achievement and therefore not one to which they wish to send their 'normal' children.

Heretofore local education authorities have determined most of the distribution of funding for special needs; it is unlikely that all schools will wish to make the same choices. Eggleston (1990) has suggested a scenario whereby many parents, even including those with children with special needs, may now seek schools that suceeed in offering what 'they know and respect'. Popular demand may well seek out schools that offer high standards in basic subjects and 'mainstream career opportunities' and conventional standards of dress and behaviour. Paradoxically, it may well be the very parents whose children might have most to gain from, say, special language provision or other special facilities who may nonetheless seek these mainstream goals in the belief that their children too should have access to what they see as the most 'privileged' type of education.

In work on parental response to the Technical and Vocational Education Initiative that attracted major special funding for schools in the 1980s (see Chapter 6) it became clear that though this new element of the secondary school curriculum offered an enhanced range of career opportunities, it was still generally less preferred by parents than the mainstream traditional academic programmes. Parents saw that a traditional academic curriculum was still being offered to high achievers in the same schools. They believed that in being offered TVEI, they were being offered second best for their children and, understandably, they wanted what they saw as 'best' (Eggleston and Sadler, 1988). It follows, therefore, that if schools and teachers are to achieve voluntary recruitment for schools with innovative curricula and teaching approaches then very considerable public relations work may have to be done.

To what extent the individual teacher can directly undertake such evangelism along with normal work with parents is a fine point of professional judgement. Overplayed, it could damage and distort the very objectives of parent–teacher co-operation; ignored, it could lead to the decline and even possible disappearance of a school.

The analogy with commercial enterprise is very close: schools are 'manufacturing' a product, selling it to consumers and must succeed if they are to survive. This is already recognized by a wide range of business management consultants offering their services to schools! Certainly there is a developing 'management literature' for schools in which management by objectives, efficiency, cost control and other commercial concepts abound.

Such business management styles are to be seen most clearly in the schools that have taken the further step on from local management of schools to opting out. The growing number of secondary and primary schools that have done this are responsible for 100 per cent of their budget, which is supplied from central rather than local government sources, again in accordance with their number of pupils. Schools that have opted early for independence from LEAs have enjoyed attractive financial incentives. The arguments for and against taking this ultimate step towards full autonomy are major issues in many school staffrooms, as are those concerning the future roles of the local education authority (Maden and Tomlinson, 1990). Indeed, there are some educationalists who see a future in which all schools have opted out and LEAs 'wither away' with only a central government supervision of state schools remaining. Another suggestion is that schools buy in any services they wish from LEAs, so that only LEAs delivering 'wanted' services would survive. The management implications are fundamental and in large schools could give rise to a new level of management posts in schools that are quite separate from teaching posts. There is already a parallel in the Health Service, where hospitals are managed not by doctors but by trained, professional hospital managers.

THE 'MICRO' ASPECTS OF TEACHER MANAGEMENT

Yet interesting and important as these 'macro' management issues are for the classroom teacher, there are also other crucial 'micro' management tasks to be undertaken. Classroom teachers are required to play a full part in the curriculum and assessment management of their schools. This involves helping to develop and implement curriculum planning across the whole school so that children's learning can be progressive and cumulative as they pass from teacher to teacher and class to class. Teachers must be involved in full and detailed consultation *between* teachers, passing not only information about children's test scores forward but also information on their learning difficulties, social background, special skills and needs and all other relevant knowledge.

In a well-managed school teachers work in a team in the interests of all the children. The enhancement of team working is the objective of the school-based in-service programmes which now take place in every school. Classroom teachers have the responsibility fully to involve themselves in this training and to ensure that it is responsive to their needs.

But much of the development of a school occurs informally, in discussion in the staffroom – often through debate and argument. Richardson (1990) points out:

> commitment often or usually occurs, if it does occur, through taking part in argument and advocacy, and pressurising and campaigning. It follows that staff need not only certain knowledge but also certain skills and qualities. For example, they need negotiating and advocacy skills, in order to be able to deal with sceptical colleagues and with (yes) sceptical and feet-dragging headteachers. And they need qualities of perseverance and courage. They will not otherwise be able to handle failure and defeat, nor mistrust and suspicion from the very people whom they are intending to help.

School management is not just about the formal curriculum but also about the informal or hidden curriculum which has been described in Chapter 4. The school in which the formal objectives are disrupted or diminished by unnoticed negative forces of the hidden curriculum is not a well-managed school. A typical example is a school where classroom organization is excellent but where playground bullying is allowed to pass unnoticed or condoned ('They've got to learn to take it' or 'It helps them to learn to fight for themselves').

AN EXAMPLE OF TEACHER MANAGEMENT: THE PROBLEM OF BULLYING

Fortunately in this, as in most other management tasks, there are now a number of sources of help for teachers so that they may be able to recognize bullying more clearly and be more aware of the misery that it causes countless pupils and its effects on their education and future life chances. Books that offer strategies include *Can I Stay In Today, Miss!* (Ross and Ryan, 1989), compiled by the Islington Teachers' Centre, and Tattum and Herbert's *Countering Bullying* (1992). There is also the moving and effective play *Only Playing Miss*, developed by the Neti-Neti Theatre Company. The script is available in book form, with workshops on bullying (Casdagli, 1990) and also as a video. There is also the excellent Central TV video, *The Trouble with Tom*, which has won the Royal Television Society prize for primary schools television. Both videos may be used effectively with children in class.

Bullying illustrates one aspect of school management which, though remote from the mandatory strategies required under legislation, is nonetheless crucial. Without such wide-ranging concerns, the objectives of the legislation and even its requirements are likely to be severely diminished in the classroom. There are many other issues, such as language policy (which involves fine judgment on the relative incidence of standard English and the use of mother tongue); equality of opportunity across race, class and gender; religious education and the varied ways in which the mandatory requirements of the Schools Advisory Committees for Religious Education (SACREs) can be developed; the arrangements for children with behavioural problems (usefully discussed by Lane, 1990); and many more. These are problems which most governing bodies will wish to be concerned with but where the detailed working out of management strategies in school and classroom will be seen as the responsibility of the professional teachers in their classrooms and in the playgrounds.

PERSONAL AND SOCIAL EDUCATION

Many teachers will try to solve such problems by building up the children's own awareness and sensitivity of the issues so that informed peer group pressure constitutes the main instrument to ensure justice and tolerance in the school. The strategies whereby young people are given explicit, organized help to become aware of interpersonal and social issues is usually called personal and social education (PSE) and features as a component of the curriculum in many schools. PSE is one of the recognized cross-curriculum themes of the National Curriculum. A typical example of a PSE programme is:

> The overall aim of the Unit is to show the way in which people often adopt unacceptable attitudes towards those who are different from themselves, to examine why this should be so, and to attempt to change any such prejudiced attitudes that exist amongst members of the group.
> It is envisaged that this Unit will form part of the PSE programme fairly early on in the pupils' school career and that it will be followed up later on in the programme by a more detailed and hard-edged examination of racism and sexism, and with a fuller consideration of the subject of the disabled.

Session One

Aim: To show that we often make judgments about people based upon superficial differences and to consider the validity of some of these judgments.

Begin the Session with a game designed to explore the similarities and differences in group members. Clear a space in the classroom and then invite the class to get into different groupings in response to a prompt. Get into groups with those who have the same:

eye colour
number of brothers and sisters
month of birth
hair colour

At the end of the game ask the children if the people in the groups were the same on each occasion. Or if there were any two of them in the same group every time. Lead on from this to try to make them realise that we all have things in common, and ways in which we are different.(Pring, 1989)

In delivering PSE explicitly or implicitly the teachers require large measures of sensitivity, perception and human understanding, and also unlimited common sense, if the pupils are to gain from the experience.

CLASSROOM MANAGEMENT

But there is another layer of management which is even more fully the responsibility of the classroom teacher. This is the management of the classroom for the creation of an effective working environment which is stimulating, supportive, unthreatening and effective for all its members.

In the preceding chapters are cited many of the areas where teachers need management skills to ensure equality of opportunity. Our prevailing concern for issues of class, race and gender is at the heart of most issues of classroom management. Writers such as Dale Spender (1980) show that, despite all intentions, teachers regularly give more attention to the boys than to the girls. Gillian Klein (1985) has shown that, again despite all good intentions, teachers regularly use racist books in their classrooms and school libraries. Twitchin (1992) makes a similar point about television programmes, including those that are used in the school, indicating the insensitivities of not just those who use such resources but also those of the producers and writers who generate them. Both are concerned about the impact of these media on children's minds. Judith Whyte (1986) has shown that the very language teachers use is sharply differentiated between boys and girls. Wright (1986) has shown similar differences in the language used by teachers to white pupils and black pupils. Again there is a very extensive literature which will further help teachers to identify these issues which will be reported in other volumes in this series.

A more general area of sensitivity is also at the heart of management. For instance, it is important that work on display in the classroom is representative of the best that all children can achieve, not just the work of an elite few. Many teachers use projects as a device for ambitious learning experiences. The impact of a project on a group or a class will vary according to the group or class ability but immense care is needed to ensure that there is genuine and satisfying achievement for all. A common experience is for a teacher to devise a class project which is attractive and exciting, such as space travel. The input of the most able children is usually creative and of very high quality, particularly if they are helped in their search for material and ideas by supportive, enthusiastic parents. Such enthusiasm and support must be welcomed as a valuable extra input to the classroom; it must never be dismissed or devalued. Yet to rely on these children to deliver a spectacular result with only minor contributions from less able children, though not without some short-term advantages for the teacher, is a means of perpetuating differences and ensuring that the test performance of children in the class reflects those differences. The problem is exacerbated when the project ends, with many children's work incomplete. It is particularly demoralizing for children when their unfinished work is destroyed at the 'tearing-up day' at the end of term. It is not difficult to see the cumulative effect on a child that a succession of unfinished, partly comprehended projects can give – and the fundamental handicap to mastery learning that these constitute. Yet, alas, these consequences of what appears to be on the face of it an appropriate teaching strategy go unnoticed all too often.

Numerous practices abound that produce the same effects: use of language in questioning, seating arrangements – these and many more are key elements in classroom management. They may seem trivial in comparison to the major issues involved in local management of schools or even in the internal organization of schools. Yet, in fact, they are crucial to a well-managed school because it is these aspects that ensure effective curriculum delivery, maximum pupil achievement and thereby the optimum result in all assessed behaviour. The success of the school, its reputation and its esteem and, above all, its recruitment pattern depend crucially on the classroom management skills of each of its teachers. Unlike many other professionals every teacher is truly a manager and likely to remain so.

SUMMARY

This chapter has reviewed the new management roles of the individual teacher in the business management strategy of contemporary schools. These are important and must be taken seriously by all teachers; to neglect them is to impair and even damage a school. Yet more fundamentally it is the small, at times almost unnoticed, aspects of management that are the real key to managerial success – the 'micro' details that underpin the 'macro' decisions. It is in making these decisions that the individual teacher's role is crucial, to children, to parents and to colleagues. If they are successful then the reinforcement of their work by children, parents and colleagues can hugely enhance their achievement.

REFERENCES

Casdagli, P. (1990) *Only Playing Miss!* Stoke-on-Trent: Trentham Books.

Eggleston, J. (1990) Anti-racist teaching and the ERA, *Multicultural Teaching*, **8**(3).

Eggleston, J. and Sadler, E. (1988) *The Participation of Ethnic Minority Pupils in TVEI*. Sheffield: The Training Agency.

Klein, G. (1985) *Reading into Racism*. London: Routledge & Kegan Paul.

Lane, D. (1990) *The Impossible Child*. Stoke-on-Trent: Trentham Books.

Maden, M. and Tomlinson, J. (1991) *Planning for School Development: A Warwickshire Case Study*. Stoke-on-Trent: Trentham Books.

Marland, M. (1989) *School Management Tasks*. London: Heinemann.

Pring, R. (1989) *The New Curriculum*. London: Cassell.

Richardson, R. (1990) *Daring to Be a Teacher*. Stoke-on-Trent: Trentham Books.

Ross, C. and Ryan, A. (eds) (1990) *Can I Stay In To-day, Miss?* Stoke-on-Trent: Trentham Books.

Spender, D. (1980) *Gender and Society*, London: Sphere.

Tattum, D. and Herbert, G. (1992) *Countering Bullying*. Stoke-on-Trent: Trentham Books.

Twitchin, J. (1992) *The Black and White Media Book* (revised edition). Stoke-on-Trent: Trentham Books.

Whyte, J. (1986) *Girls into Science and Technology*. London: Routledge.

Wright, C. (1986) School processes: an ethnographic study, in Eggleston, J., Dunn, D. and Anjali, M. (eds) *Education for Some*. Stoke-on-Trent: Trentham Books.

RECOMMENDED READING

Planning for School Development: A Warwickshire Case Study by Margaret Maden and John Tomlinson (Stoke-on-Trent: Trentham Books, 1991) is a frank account by a chief education officer and a former chief education officer (now Director of the Institute of Education at the University of Warwick) which encapsulates 'insider' thinking on the major changes taking place in the running of schools.

Can I Stay In To-day, Miss?, edited by C. Ross and A. Ryan (Stoke-on-Trent: Trentham Books, 1989), was written by a group of Islington teachers. It is a moving account of how the misery of playground bullying could be stopped, with excellent pictures that also tell the story. It indicates just how vital is this aspect of a teacher's management role.

Michael Marland, *School Management Tasks* (London: Heinemann, 1988) is an excellent practical guide by one of the most successful headteachers in Britain. Very readable.

Gillian Klein, *Reading into Racism* (London: Routledge & Kegan Paul, 1985) offers yet another perspective on classroom management: the choice of literature. It is particularly good on the criteria teachers can use, and is by no means confined to racist criteria alone.

The School Management Task Force's *Developing School Management* (London: HMSO, 1991) is directed at heads, but this is no reason why beginning teachers should not read it too. Up to date, informative and concise.

CHAPTER 8

Conclusion

Throughout, this book has emphasized the power of the individual teacher. Perhaps no other professionals have such remarkable power as classroom teachers. In the privacy of the classroom or teaching area they have virtually total control over the school lives of their pupils for a series of lessons or, more usually, for the greater part of the year or of a subject area for a number of years. Though they are subject to supervision of senior teachers, inspectors and advisers and controlled by national legislation there is a vast amount of personal responsibility that is, and can only, be exercised by the teacher.

The book has discussed the exercise of this power and responsibility in curriculum, assessment, management and career formation. But above all it has shown that in ensuring equality of opportunity across race, class and gender it is individual teachers who are supreme and it is through their sensitivity, perception and subtlety that the lives of all children may be enhanced or diminished. Virtually every outcome of the school springs from the quality of the classroom experience, not least the school's success in winning the support of parents, which is becoming more crucial. The introduction to this book asserted that new legislation can help teachers to teach and children to learn. But this vital link between legislation and achievement is the quality of the teacher.

Unquestionably schools, and teachers, do make a difference, with or without legislation. It is estimated, for instance, that the knowledge possessed by a school leaver with 5 Cs at GCSE in 1990 would have been sufficient to earn a respectable degree at Oxford or Cambridge in 1900. Schools and teachers must have played a major part in the change!

There is no shortage of evidence of teacher achievement. The HMI report on the first year of Mathematics in the National Curriculum presented a glowing account of the achievements of teachers in a difficult year (HMI, 1991). Fortunately there is a widespread recognition of the work of teachers. Kenneth Clarke, the then Secretary of State for Education, addressing the North of England Education Conference on 4 January 1991, commented:

> Education is a person-to-person service totally dependent on the quality and commitment of those who teach. Systems and buildings are important but they matter less than the teachers in a successful education service. We must ensure that our teachers are trained and supported to have the skills and knowledge to meet the new demands placed upon them by a more sophisticated service seeking to stretch all our children to the limits of their talents.

It may even be that at times teachers diminish their own recognition. Only a few months earlier Baroness Young, a former Education Minister, was reported in *The Times* (21 September 1990): 'She told the Headmasters' Conference in Aberdeen that too many teachers talked down the profession and refused to set high standards for themselves or their pupils. Teachers had tried to dissuade her own daughter from joining the profession.'

Yet the success and achievement of school, however measured or presented, cannot be fully known even by the most assiduous teacher. An American fable of a rich jade collector makes the point well. The story concerns a wealthy American who sought a safe and prestigious way of retaining his wealth in an inflation-prone society. His friends advised him that he should collect jade. 'It doesn't lose its value and you can show it to your friends and impress them.' But, they went on, 'beware of fake jade – you must get the real stuff'. As a result his path led him to a course of lessons from a distinguished jade specialist. On the first lesson he was shown into the expert's study and invited to contemplate a piece of jade. For the whole hour no further words were exchanged and at the end the specialist bowed and left. The American collector was furious; he complained to his friends that he had spent $1,000 on the lesson and that he had been told nothing. His friends advised him to have patience and to persist with the remaining nine lessons. He did so, but on each occasion the same thing happened and on each occasion his frustration grew more intense. However, he was again counselled to stay to the end of the course when, at the tenth lesson, all would be revealed. But at the end of the tenth lesson he was equally outraged because again the same pattern had been followed by the specialist. His final outraged comment was 'Not only has this guy told me nothing yet again, but on this occasion he even had the cheek to put out a piece of dud jade for me to look at.'

This story embodies one of the fundamental truths of teaching. Few people realize fully what and when they are learning; the real evidence of classroom learning commonly occurs after schooling has ended, when the teachers are no longer around to assess, let alone take credit for the achievement. If any teachers doubt this let them again be reminded to follow some of their ex-pupils into the street, club or pub and listen as they argue fluently and with sophistication about the merits and complexity of 'their team'.

Of course, examples such as this indicate that, for many young people, leisure applications of knowledge are more attractive than work applications. Norman Fowler (*The Times*, 7 February 1991) commented: 'The British workforce is a sleeping giant. Or, perhaps more precisely, a giant whose energies and capacities are too rarely fully realised or released at work. Those energies are left to find release in other ways – programming the video recorder, or improving the performance of cars or motorbikes.'

The challenge for teachers seeking to develop enterprise education is unmistakable. Yet teachers must not over-react to such comments: education for leisure is also an important objective. Though important, occupational and examination success can never be the sole or even the major evidence of teachers' achievement. Maximizing opportunity is a crucial goal for teachers, but the availability of occupational success is determined outside the classroom and in most modern societies is in restricted supply. Teachers must offer more than occupational opportunities if they are honest in motivating their pupils.

Here we are back to the concepts of the teacher's self-assessment that we sighted at the beginning of this book. Ultimately teachers must be able to assess the true worth of their curriculum, their teaching styles, their management capability, their delivery of equal opportunities and ultimately the life opportunities achieved by the pupils. Only the teachers themselves can do it wholly; any system of tests can offer only partial, and often distorted, evidence. Perhaps the most fundamental message of the book is that more than any other professional the teacher has to be inner-directed rather than other-directed. This book has also sought to emphasize that children are different, and that the teacher must respond to this difference. Robin Richardson makes this clear in his inspiring *Daring to Be a Teacher* (1990):

> Each child is individual and unique, of course, and has her own distinct unfolding. But also all are members of groups, collectives, communities: each belongs to a social class, an ethnic group, a religious tradition, a 'race', a gender, a local neighbourhood. Therefore the futures of collective identities are at stake in education, not those of individuals only. And it is not only the future which is at risk, but the present moment too: life, liberty and the pursuit of happiness this day, this week, this year. And further, you yourself are in danger – you the teacher, you the back-up administrator.

But he also emphasizes the stress and difficulties of being a teacher:

You have a duty to take care of yourself, and your self includes your body (for the body is not just that thing which carries your head around), and also your spirit (which is not just that strange place you sometimes visit, without being adequately consulted, in your dreams).

This book has sought to show ways to achieve this and so to help readers to respond to this ultimate challenge. Teachers always make a difference, but that difference must be enhancing and positive, not diminishing and negative – for all pupils.

REFERENCES

Her Majesty's Inspectorate (1991) *Mathematics, Key Stages 1 & 3: A Report on the First Year*. London: HMSO.

Richardson, R. (1990) *Daring to Be a Teacher*. Stoke-on-Trent: Trentham Books.